S

Keeper
of
CEOs'
CONSCIENCE

SUN TZU

THE KEEPER of CEOs' CONSCIENCE

KHOO KHENG-HOR
Bestselling author of SUN TZU & MANAGEMENT

Any book can teach you
about managing others, but
Sun Tzu's *Art of War*
is especially about managing
oneself in order to
secure victories

Pelanduk
Publications

Published by
Pelanduk Publications (M) Sdn. Bhd.,
24 Jalan 20/16A, 46300 Petaling Jaya,
Selangor Darul Ehsan,
Malaysia.

All correspondence to:
Pelanduk Publications (M) Sdn. Bhd.,
P.O. Box 8265, 46785 Kelana Jaya,
Selangor Darul Ehsan, Malaysia.

Perpustakaan Negara Malaysia   Cataloguing-in-Publication Data

Khoo, Kheng-Hor, 1956-
    Sun Tzu: the keeper of CEOs' conscience / Khoo Kheng-Hor.
    Includes Index
    ISBN 967-978-595-5
    ISBN 967-978-594-7 (pbk.)
    1. Chief executive officers. 2. Executives. I. Title.
    658.409

Printed by
Teknik Pelanduk Sdn. Bhd.

Dedication

This book is dedicated to my wife, Judy, who, has been the keeper of my conscience throughout my climb up the corporate ladder until Sun Tzu came on board as co-keeper.

Contents

The Author

As a business executive, consultant, author and speaker, Khoo Kheng-Hor has been described as a contemporary interpreter of Sun Tzu's treatise, the *Art of War*. He has been interviewed on television, radio, newspapers and magazines for his creative interpretations of Sun Tzu's war principles for use, not only in strategic management, but also in specific areas of management such as marketing, customer service and human resource management, as well as corporate politics.

He now lives in Singapore with his wife, Judy, and besides running Stirling Training & Management Consultants Pte Ltd, his own firm which assists clients in planning and implementing strategies and motivating their executives through his specially developed *"Management, the Sun Tzu Way"* programs, he also writes a monthly column for *Asia-21* and lectures part-time on strategic management for the Singapore Institute of Management's external degree programs.

His other books are *War At Work: Applying Sun Tzu's Art of War in Today's Business World*, *Sun Tzu's Art of War* (a translation), *Personnel Management Manual*, *Sun Tzu and Management*, *Personnel Policies* and *Applying Sun Tzu's Art of War in Corporate Politics*.

Preface

IT ALL STARTED in late-1994 when Mr Lin Cheng Ton, the principal and CEO of Nanyang Polytechnic in Singapore, invited me to tea.

In between hot sips, Mr Lin asked me whether I would care to address some 60 CEOs on the subject of how to apply Sun Tzu's *Art of War* in today's management. Naturally, I choked and spluttered over my cup of tea. Even though I am a much-sought-after speaker for public and in-house seminars on my pet subject, the application of Sun Tzu's *Art of War* to contemporary management, still I was quite taken aback by Mr Lin's invitation. Who am I to teach management at such an august gathering of no lesser personages than CEOs? Besides, by my reckoning, most CEOs are themselves, already experts in the *Art of War* even if they may not consciously be aware of the actual sayings of Sun Tzu.

But then, having been taught by my late father, Khoo Ah Leng, never to quit without a try, I recollected Sun Tzu's words that:

> *A wise general considers both the advantages and disadvantages opened to him. When considering the advantages, he makes his plans feasible; when considering the disadvantages, he finds ways to extricate himself from the difficulties.*

The advantages in addressing the 60 CEOs would mean an opportunity for networking and more business although the disadvantage would be the extreme pressure in facing such a high-level (and thereby more critical) crowd. It was then that I hit upon the idea of using the theme: SUN TZU – the Keeper of CEOs' Conscience.

Why this Theme?

As CEOs are also human and therefore prone to make mistakes like anyone else, they stand an even greater risk up there since everyone else, in their lower stations would not feel 'big' enough to point out the mistakes of their CEOs. As the *Art of War* contains much wisdom in highlighting the potential pitfalls facing generals of old, it would be as applicable to CEOs of this modern world. Besides, since I am only acting as a 'medium', passing on Sun Tzu's words of wisdom to remind CEOs of their follies or would-be follies, no CEO's feathers would be unnecessarily ruffled by what I have to say.

The result: my talk held on 18 February 1995 was a success, with several CEOs complimenting me and subsequently inviting me to give in-house talks to their executives. One of them, Mr Paul Chan, the then General Manager and Director of Hewlett-

Packard Singapore (Sales) Pte Ltd, even had his team of managers from the South Asian region flown in to hear my interpretations of Sun Tzu's *Art of War* which they found to be "useful and applicable to our (HP) environment".

The theme was again repeated successfully at the 12th Asian Association of Management Organization's conference from 6-8 November 1995 when I was invited to be one of the guest speakers. By then, I had already compiled my papers into almost two thirds of this book. Thus, when PHP International, the publisher of the then *Intersect Japan-Asia* (now changed to *Asia-21*) subsequently invited me to write a monthly column on this theme, beginning January 1996, I decided to release parts of my intended book to test reader's reaction. The feedback provided *Asia-21*'s editor, Ms Catherine Khoo, was positive as there were requests from other publications for reprints.

Now that I have completed the remaining chapters to publish this book (my seventh published so far), I must record my gratitude for the direct and indirect encouragement given to me Mr Lin Cheng Ton, Mr Paul Chan, Dr Tan Jin Hee, Mr Yoshi Ogura, Ms Catherine Khoo, and the many other CEOs who had invited me to talk to their executives.

Khoo Kheng-Hor

Introducing
Sun Tzu
and The
Art Of War

WHAT HAS A 2,500-year-old Chinese military strategist to do with being a keeper of a CEO's conscience?

The answer: Plenty. The war principles as found in Sun Tzu's book, *Art of War*, has much to offer in safeguarding a CEO from the many moralistic pitfalls of his high office.

To understand the man and his work, it is appropriate to narrate the following story which is familiar to many Chinese (and an even greater number of Japanese):

> Around 500BC when Sun Tzu, a native of Qi, wrote *Art of War*, Prince He Lu of Wu was so impressed by what he read that he granted him an audience.
>
> The Prince who had read all of Sun Tzu's 13 chapters on warfare, wanted to test Sun Tzu's skill in drilling troops, using women. Sun Tzu was prepared to face this test and Prince He Lu sent for 180 ladies from his palace.

Sun Tzu divided them into two companies, each headed by one of the Prince's two favorite concubines. After arming all the women with spears, Sun Tzu asked: "Do you know where is front and back, right and left?"

When all the women replied in the affirmative, Sun Tzu went on to instruct them thus: "When I command 'front', you must face directly ahead; 'turn left', you must face to the left; 'turn right', you must face to the right; 'back', you must turn right around towards your back".

As all the women assented, Sun Tzu laid out the executioner's weapons to show his seriousness on discipline and began the drill to the sounds of drum beats and shouts of commands. None of the women moved and instead they burst into laughter.

Sun Tzu patiently told them that commands which are unclear and, therefore, not thoroughly understood would be the commander's fault, and proceeded to instruct them once more.

When the drums were beaten a second time and the commands repeated, the women again burst into fits of laughter. This time, Sun Tzu said: "Commands which are unclear and not thoroughly understood would be the commander's fault. But when commands are clear and the soldiers none-theless do not carry them out, then it is the fault of their officers". So saying, he ordered both concu-bines who were heading the two companies out for execution.

The Prince, who was witnessing the drill from a raised pavilion, on seeing his favorite concubines sent out for execution, was greatly alarmed and quickly sent an aide with the message: "I believe the general is capable of drilling troops. Without these two concubines, my food and drink will be tasteless. It is my desire that they be spared".

Sun Tzu replied that having received the royal commission to lead troops in the field, he can disregard any of the Ruler's commands as he sees fit. Accordingly, he had the two concubines beheaded as an example and thereafter appointed two women next in line to take their places as Company Leaders.

Thereafter, the drill proceeded smoothly with every women obediently turning left, right, front or back; kneeling or rising, with perfect precision, without laughing or uttering any dissent.

Sun Tzu then sent a messenger to the Prince requesting him to inspect the troops which he declared as having been properly drilled and disciplined, and prepared even to go through fire and water for the Prince.

When the Prince declined, Sun Tzu remarked: "The Prince is only fond of words which he cannot put into practice".

Greatly ashamed by what he heard, and recognizing Sun Tzu's ability, Prince He Lu promptly appointed Sun Tzu as the supreme commander of the Wu armies.

In 506BC, Sun Tzu led five expeditions against the State of Zhu which had regarded Wu as a vassal. He defeated the armies of Zhu and forced his way into the Zhu capital, Ying-du, while King Zhao fled, leaving his State on the verge of extermination.

For almost 20 years thereafter, the armies of Wu continued to be victorious against those of its neighbors, the States of Qi, Qin and Yue. However, after Sun Tzu's death, his successors failed to follow his precepts and suffered defeat after defeat until 473BC when the kingdom became extinct.

But anyone who lacks consideration and treats the enemy with contempt and disdain will only end up being captured himself.

天峰無意而自見敵者必擒於人

1

Arrogance is the Root of All CEOs' Problems

MANY WRITERS HAVE recently been turning to Sun Tzu's *Art of War*, a Chinese military treatise written about 2,500 years ago, for its relevance to fighting in today's corporate and marketing 'battlefields'. As a result, more Sun Tzu's books have invaded the bookshops and even more businessmen and executives have been trying to draw lessons and inspiration from the philosophy of Sun Tzu.

Since Sun Tzu's *Art of War* abounds with many reminders of the pitfalls facing the general or ruler (we can simply view these two parties in contemporary management as managers and the owners respectively), it is my hope that more CEOs could benefit from his treatise. While it is not for me to teach management to CEOs, I can however use Sun Tzu's war principles to alert them on some of the potential pitfalls peculiar to being a CEO. This is because the moment we reached senior management level such as the exalted position of CEO, we would more often than not, lapse into making mistakes which we normally would not when struggling to climb the corporate ladder.

Call it Arrogance, Conceit or Pride

To kick off this self-exploration of our conscience through Sun Tzu, I will touch on a primary pitfall awaiting most CEOs as they make it to the top of their organization – arrogance.

It is not unusual that after having struggled for so long for this moment to be named CEO, we may feel a little smug (which in itself, is an understatement) and take to this line of thought: "Surely I'm the greatest, for how else could I have made it". At this stage, chances are high that in our newly acquired sense of omnipotence, we will believe all our decisions are definitely the right ones. Indeed, it is impossible to be a successful manager without believing we are better than others.

But as Sun Tzu has warned:

> *In battle, having more soldiers will not necessarily secure victory. Never advance by relying blindly on the strength of military power alone. It is sufficient to concentrate our strength, estimate the enemy's position and seek his capture. But anyone who lacks consideration and treats the enemy with contempt and disdain will only end up being captured himself.*

Sun Tzu's words here are intended to shake us out of our self-centredness. While it is true that much of our strength comes from within ourselves, we still need a more open mind, especially in relation to the outside world and thus have to further search for success outside ourselves. It is such self-centredness that led most people who have made it to the top, to thereafter extol hard work (their industriousness), business acumen (their cleverness), and determination (their strength of mind and character) as ingredients of their success. These people would seldom credit luck (or divine intervention as some more religious or humble ones would admit) or being in the right place at the right time. Management guru Tom Peters has been more honest when he says: "I don't like the whole notion of career planning. I've never had a formula, never had a life plan. I only take advantage of luck whenever it comes. Luck is 98 percent of the deal".

Over-belief in our Strength

Too much blind faith in our own strength is dangerous. In forgetting the element of luck, and believing too much in our own omnipotence, we can also develop the tendency to forget those people who matters in our continued success – our customers and our employees.

Take selling, for example. We do not make a sale all by ourselves, especially not in our role as CEOs. Rather, a sale is made only if there are people who are willing to buy from us. It is certainly worthwhile for arrogant CEOs who believe too much in themselves and/or their products to learn from John Akers, who, when as CEO of IBM, personally got involved in meeting with customer groups, promising IBM's readiness to listen to their complaints and suggestions. Much closer to home, we could also take a cue from Konosuke Matsushita whose rise from poverty and obscurity to become the head of one of the world's most powerful corporations, only made him more humble and down-to-earth in his dealings.

Moreover, the actual selling process is really in the hands of our sales personnel. In our posh offices or in the equally posh boardrooms, we may talk at length about the importance of customer service and thereafter put up many lofty directives. But if, in our arrogance, we have failed to consider the feelings of our sales personnel and thus neglected their motivation, all it take would be a few of them not delighting our customers out there, and soon all those lofty ideals will come to nought.

Expectations of Greater Rewards

Just as it is impossible to be a successful manager without believing we are better than others, it is equally impossible in that state of mind, not to believe we deserve greater rewards than others. This is the reason why CEOs tend to incur more expenses in their respective organization than the other employees. After all, they do need a bigger office room (which must, unlike those of other executives, have a high-quality leather sofa set, thus justifying the additional floor space), more presentable (and therefore expensive) furniture, a bigger (and of course, newer) car, etc., besides a salary that is not only much higher than those of the other employees in his organization but must be comparable (meaning a bit higher) than other CEOs in other organizations. Newly-appointed CEOs often cannot wait for their turns to jump into this spend-spend-spend syndrome in their need to keep up image commensurating their newly acquired status. In his time, Sun Tzu has observed:

> *Thus, the general who advances without coveting fame and withdraws without fearing disgrace, but whose sole intention is to protect the people and serve his ruler, is the precious jewel of the State.*

CEOs who are the 'precious jewels' of their States would be those who are careful not to cultivate arrogance. For them, it is always the organization's interest that comes first. Whatever they do is for the best of their organization rather than in service of their own personal interest. They are human like the rest of us, and therefore given to a passion for good living but the only difference is that they are more self-disciplined which is in keeping with what Sun Tzu advocated:

The good commander seeks virtues and goes about disciplining himself according to the laws so as to effect control over his success.

In cultivating self-discipline, these CEOs would spend only when it is necessary for them to do so. A business trip may thus entail merely a business-class flight and a comfortable room in a reputable hotel rather than something fanciful like chartering (or even buying and maintaining) an entire aeroplane or booking an expensive hotel suite unless there is a crucial need, e.g. to impress certain people whom one is dealing with. Most of the CEOs I know would rather fly business than first-class. As one told me: "Unless the flight is long, and first-class could give that extra comfort, I would rather go business-class since the only real difference today is the price of the fare".

Anger as a Measure

Arrogance can at times be measured by the frequency of our outburst of temper in our high office as CEO. On many occasions, Sun Tzu has warned about anger:

> *If a general cannot control his anger and sends his soldiers to swarm up the walls like ants, then one-third of his troops will be killed without taking the city...*

and,

> *...There are five dangerous faults which a general should not have in his character... a quick temper which enables you to make him look foolish...*

and again,

> *...No ruler should put troops into the field because he is angry; no general should fight because he is resentful. Move when there is benefit to be gained, quit when there is no more advantage. For an angry man can later become happy, a resentful man become pleased, but a kingdom once destroyed can never be restored nor the dead be brought back to life.*

Even then, it is not surprising to find CEOs who are given to frequent displays of temper. Arrogance is again very much at the root because the more arrogant a CEO becomes, the more he is assailed with events that he perceives as having slighted him. The more his conceit grows, the more daily events appear to conspire against his personal grandeur.

As one CEO told me: "At the time I didn't realize it but my life evolved around petty issues when I should be focused on the big and important ones. One morning, I was so annoyed to read of one of my managers giving his comments in the newspapers on what books he had read that I shouted at my secretary for not being able to get me a lunch table at my favorite restaurant. In retrospect, I was annoyed because in my self-perceived grandeur, I felt I should be the one being interviewed instead of my subordinate. Hence, when the restaurant was so fully booked that even I could not get a table, I just could not accept that such a thing could happen to me... it kind of burst my bubble of self-esteem. So, unconsciously, I shifted the blame to my secretary, making out that it was her incompetence... not my lack of importance."

Arrogance and Misinformation

Just as anger could be measured by the frequency of temper outburst, there appears to be a high positive correlation between arrogance and misinformation. Like dictatorial kings of ancient times who rarely get honest opinions from their sycophant ministers, arrogant CEOs today seldom get honest views from their fearful staff. Let us regard information – regardless of open views or covert intelligence – in Sun Tzu's observation:

> *The relationship between the commander and his secret agent is more intimate than all others in the army. The rewards given to secret agents are more liberal than any other given. The confidentiality given to secret operations is greater than for other matters. Only the wise and sagely, benevolent and just, can use secret agents. Only he who is sensitive and subtle can get the truth of their reports.*

Hence, the more arrogant the CEO, the more the layers will filter out the bad news and pass along only the good news since nobody wants to be blamed for bursting the CEO's egoistic bubble. And when things start to go bad, the arrogant CEO is often the last one to know.

If you know yourself and know your enemy, in a hundred battles, you will never fear the result. When you know yourself but not your enemy, your chances of winning or losing are equal. If you know neither yourself nor your enemy, you are certain to be in danger in every battle.

知己忠彼者
百戰百勝

不知彼而忠己
一勝一負

不知彼不忠己
每戰必殆

2
After Arrogance Comes Ignorance

HAVING SHARED WITH you on the pitfall of arrogance in CEOship, we shall next look at the danger of ignorance which is a natural companion of arrogance.

This is what Sun Tzu warned:

> *When a general fails to size up his enemy and uses inferior force to engage a larger one, or weak troops to attack the strong, or neglects to place picked men in the front ranks, the result is a rout.*

An ignorant CEO can be a most pitiful creature. Just imagine, pitting inferior or weak troops against the strong?!!! Even a primary school kid knows better than to pick on the bigger and stronger boys for a quarrel. So how about a head of a corporation going against the business trends or taking on a stronger competitor?

Considering that CEOs have assiduously struggled a good part of their lives to make it to their high positions, how is it then that they could lapse into this pitfall of ignorance at their peak?

The Link to Arrogance

Time and again, when advocating strategies in his book, Sun Tzu mentioned arrogance:

> *Hold out baits to lure the enemy; feign disorder and strike him... pretend weakness so that he may become arrogant.*

The intention of which is to caution against arrogance:

> *...anyone who lacks consideration and treats the enemy with contempt and disdain will only end up being captured himself.*

Hence, some of those ignorant CEOs deserve no sympathy. As I have written in the last chapter, like dictatorial kings of ancient times who rarely get honest opinions from their sycophant ministers, arrogant CEOs today seldom get honest views from their fearful staff. And the more arrogant they are, the more the layers will filter out the bad news and pass along only the good news so much so that such CEOs are constantly kept in the dark on whatever is happening since nobody wants to be blamed for spoiling their optimistic views. Ignorance thus is the outcome of arrogance. In this way, you can say an ignorant CEO often has his own over-bloated ego to blame.

Of Meddling CEOs

This is what Sun Tzu warned when pointing out that of the three ways whereby a ruler could bring misfortune upon his army, the first would be:

> *By commanding an army to advance or retreat, when ignorant on whether to advance or retreat. This is called 'hobbling the army'.*

There is indeed a tendency for CEOs to make decisions arbitrarily on relatively insignificant matters which they are not familiar about and which ought to be left to proficient executives down the line. I have encountered one such CEO who personally disputed the purchase of a low-priced facsimile machine which was badly needed to replace an older slower machine. The old machine often requires the person using it to stand by for some time painstakingly feeding in sheets of documents one by one. The CEO never once considered the bunching effect of periodic high transmission or the need to facilitate communications with clients (thus losing business opportunities). As a result, he was in effect spending several thousand dollars worth of his and other executives' time, to interfere with a perfectly justifiable decision lower down to buy a machine worth much less than their executive time.

When Ignorance is the Result of Niggardliness

Although the CEO mentioned in the last paragraph may be meddling on account of thriftiness, the entire issue is still too petty and hardly justifies his interference. This could be Sun Tzu's intention when he observes:

*He who faces an enemy for many years to struggle for
the victory that can be decided in a single day and yet
remains ignorant of the enemy's position because he be-
grudges giving ranks, honors and a few hundred pieces
of gold, is totally without humanity. Such a man is no
leader, no help to his ruler, no master of victory.*

I can recall many other examples though I shall offer only
two here:

In one company, the CEO wanted his managers to be well-
informed on any development in the market. It thus struck me as
most strange to find his company subscribing to only three sets
of newspapers to be read and passed on by each of the twelve
managers, i.e. a newspaper to be shared by four managers. The
company even has a rubber stamp made for stamping on the
newspaper to allow the managers concerned to sign his name to
acknowledge having read the newspaper for the day before passing on to the next person. It is no wonder that none of the managers shared the boss's enthusiasm for them to be well-informed
managers who could contribute ideas. As one of them put it: "As
we can readily afford to buy our own newspaper, by doing that
sort of thing, our CEO has kind of cheapened us... he doesn't
consider each of us as an individual whose dignity ought to be re-
spected".

Then, there was the CEO who would say "Give me three
months of continuous profitability" or "Let me see incremental
sales of 20 per cent" whenever any of his managers were to request for capital expenditure in equipment to facilitate their
business. When I think of the lost productivity through im-
proved efficiency, I cannot help being reminded of a man pray-
ing at the roadside shrine of his deity: "Please let me strike this

month's lottery and I shall come back with roasted chicken and wine as offerings ..."

The Ability to Listen

How then could you, as a CEO, avoid this pitfall of ignorance? Firstly, be extremely honest with yourself and see if you can recognize yourself as a person who has 'seen it all' and thus no longer need to be told, or worse, as someone who only likes his own views and not those of others. As Sun Tzu summed up in one of his most famous sayings:

> *If you know yourself and know your enemy, in a hundred battles, you will never fear the result. When you know yourself but not your enemy, your chances of winning or losing are equal. If you know neither yourself nor your enemy, you are certain to be in danger in every battle.*

If you have been guilty of the said follies, it may still be timely to bring about the much needed changes. Even if you are not guilty of any of the said follies, it is still wise to pay heed to Sun Tzu's advice:

> *The good commander seeks virtues and goes about disciplining himself according to the laws so as to effect control over his success.*

One of the disciplines which a CEO need is: learn to listen – not just to things you would like to hear but also unpleasant things as well. When I first met Klaus Jacobs, the chairman of Adia SA, I deliberately ignored the advice given me earlier by those who claimed to know him: "Don't talk too much but just listen to him as he doesn't like people to talk too much". In my view, as the head of a corporation which has over 1,900 offices worldwide, if he doesn't stop to listen, then he is not the man I would like to work with. Thus, in our first meeting, I did most of the talking which gave me the opportunity to learn something more of the man – he took notes on his small notebook! And within a week after he had returned to Zurich in Switzerland, I got an action letter from him with very pointed advice... which showed me he did not only listen but he analyzed everything I had told him. Indeed, this was the very same man who initiated the 'dawn raid' against Rowntree Plc on 13 April 1988.

Empower your Subordinates

Another approach is to develop the best in your subordinates through empowerment. Hence, even if you, as the CEO, do not know, you can still benefit from subordinates who know. But it is really sad to find not many CEOs could see the power which could come from empowering their managers. As a newly appointed general manager found out after joining a retail chain, every one of his actions must have the 'green light' of the group managing director. Even though the latter has issued a circular stating every key executive's authority limit to approve capital expenditure, he can still revoke any purchase order which has already been sent to the vendor. Just imagine the general manager's surprise and embarrassment when a purchase order approved by him for the purchase of a low-priced computer was revoked by his boss and has to be retracted from the vendor. It is not surprising that he lost all his initial enthusiasm to do a great job for his company and left after about five months.

Even though it was 500BC, Sun Tzu had already discovered the power of empowerment as he has written:

> *Put your men in positions where there is no escape and even when facing death, they will not run... Thus, without the need of supervision, they will be alert, and without being asked, they will support their general; without being ordered, they will trust him.*

The effective CEO therefore seeks to create such situations for victory and realizes that depriving subordinates of the power required to do a job well is certainly not good management practice.

The Price of Knowledge

A well-informed CEO (and his well-informed state is due to some extent to his having well-informed managers) is the key to an organization's success. In his wisdom, Sun Tzu recognized the need to cultivate a desire for knowledge:

> *The enlightened ruler and the wise general can subdue the enemy whenever they move and they can achieve superhuman feats because they have foreknowledge.*

Such knowledge however does not mean having access to voluminous information. Instead of being helpful, too much information may be over-pressurizing. This is what Sun Tzu must have meant when he writes about concentration of force:

> *In battle, having more soldiers will not necessarily secure victory. Never advance by relying blindly on the strength of military power. It is sufficient to concentrate our strength, estimate the enemy's position and seek his capture.*

As soldiers are a form of resource, we can use this term to refer to other resources as well. Thus, in this case, we can refer to the resource of information where despite having more, will not necessarily ensure victory. The aim here is for quality rather than quantity. And like all things of quality, a price tag is inevitable. Hence, do not be stingy about the price.

It is a principle of war that we do not assume the enemy will not come, but instead we must be prepared for his coming; not to presume he will not attack but instead to make our own position unassailable.

故用兵之法

無恃其不來

恃吾有以待也

無恃其不攻

恃吾有所不可攻也

3
Arrogance Plus Ignorance Equal Complacency

IN THE LAST two chapters, you have seen the pitfalls of arrogance and ignorance. A combination of these two pitfalls will result in complacency.

Sun Tzu has given this warning:

It is a principle of war that we do not assume the enemy will not come, but instead we must be prepared for his coming; not to presume he will not attack but instead to make our own position unassailable.

When we have not yet made it, but are instead struggling to scale the corporate ladder, our senses are somehow more alert to any or all possible issues or problems which may jeopardize our journey upwards. Hence, while on the climb, we tend to be more careful about not making mistakes. But the moment we make it into the CEO's softchair amidst mahogany-walled panels, all too often we tend to be seduced into letting our guard down. The rationale is: "I've made it! I don't have to struggle that hard anymore".

This would be the same mistake most people make when entering into marriages. A man may have won the heart of his sweetheart but marriage is not the end. Rather, it is just the beginning. If he does not work as hard (if not more) at making the marriage last, then he risks the marriage going to the rocks in a very short time. Similarly, making it to the top management position is really the beginning, not the end.

The Quest for Competitive Advantage

Any complacency on the part of a CEO could very well prove disastrous to his organization. Since many management gurus have talked at length about competitive advantage, let us look at the development of competitive advantage.

In competing with one another, businesses search for an advantage that will attract customers to them and away from competitors. But a complacent CEO will be so relaxed that he will not actively search for such an advantage. Instead, he will allow his competitors find the opportunity to get at his firm. Sun Tzu observed:

> *Invincibility lies in one's own hands, but the enemy's vulnerability is of his own making. Thus, those skilled in war can make themselves invincible but the enemy's vulnerability is provided only by the enemy himself.*

The US automobile industry offers a good example. In the 1970s, American automakers continued to roll out big petrol-guzzlers even after the Arab oil embargo had consumers switching to the smaller and more fuel-efficient Japanese cars. In their complacency, the American CEOs further neglected or were simply not interested in markets such as Southeast Asia. As a result, the Japanese had all the opportunities and time to develop the said market without being threatened by their stronger Western counterparts. And where there were some competition (more from the European automakers), such tended to be scattered or very segmented and thus not much of an obstacle to the Japanese. The latter have since been enjoying an advantage which could be summed up by Sun Tzu in the following:

> *That you may march a thousand li (one li = half mile) without exhaustion is due to the country being free of enemy troops. You can be sure of taking what you attack if you attack those places which are undefended.*

Those CEOs who want to develop the competitive edge must thus avoid this pitfall of complacency. They must instead have the willingness to learn about and exploit opportunities. Or they must be so self-disciplined that they are ready at all times to look critically at themselves. This latter approach would be in keeping with Sun Tzu's exhortation that:

> *The good commander seeks virtues and goes about disciplining himself according to the laws so as to effect control over his success.*

Or to put it more directly: be daring to attack yourself. As Dr Willis Carrier of Carrier Air-conditioners has said: "The greatest challenge is to obsolete one's triumph".

Complacency in Successful Corporations

Like the leaders who drive them, successful corporations are easy prey to conceit, which helps create their own failure. These

CEOs who determine the corporate direction in part, should thus shoulder the ultimate responsibility. Sun Tzu has always been relentless in his censure of the man in command:

> *When troops are inclined to flee, to insubordinate against commands, distressed, disorganized or defeated, it is the fault of the general as none of these calamities arises from natural causes.*

Many CEOs have been known to have refused to block strong competitive moves because their egos got in the way. Or worse, they allow their egos to carry them away into attacking a strong competitor, a move which Sun Tzu warned:

> *Do not engage an enemy whose banners are in perfect order or whose troops are arrayed in an impressive formation.*

It is heartening then to find a corporate giant like IBM, when under the leadership of CEO John Akers, embarking on a strategy involving nothing less than reinventing IBM. As IBM then was so relentless on attacking itself, its customers were therefore assured that Big Blue would constantly be introducing new and better products that make IBM's own products obsolete.

When reading Hewlett-Packard's annual report for 1994, I was delighted by its CEO Lew Platt's closing message: "We start 1995 with important strengths: technology leadership, outstanding product programs, excellent presence in the reseller channel and a good position in emerging markets. However, we expect the competitive environment to remain unforgiving, and we're determined to avoid complacency in any form".

Neutral Strategies

For obvious reasons, I have always been wary on the use of neutral strategy which some firms are fond of adopting. Two variations of neutral strategy being:

1. holding, i.e. attempting to continue doing what has been done all the while so as to keep a steady rate of growth albeit at slower rate than the external environment; and
2. harvesting, i.e. aiming to generate cash for the corporation or shareholders while reducing further investment.

Unless it is only a temporary solution, i.e. stop and observe the situation for a while before deciding on the next course of action, or there is no other alternative, the adoption of such strategies smirks of complacency on the part of the CEO, e.g. "Why change or tamper with success since our firm has already been doing well all these years?" Or could it be that the firm is simply unaware that it is not keeping up with the competition and so continues on a neutral course? The answer is more likely to be found in the fact that people are generally uncomfortable with change. And the more established an organization, the more comfortable the management will be with the way things are done and so are reluctant to change.

But change is all important and has been advocated by Sun Tzu ever since he first wrote the *Art of War* some 2,500 years ago for he says:

> *Thus, when I win a victory, I do not repeat the tactics but respond to circumstances in limitless ways.*

He goes on to elaborate, using water as the metaphor:

As water shapes its flow according to the ground, an army wins by relating to the enemy it faces. And just as water retains no constant shape, in war there will be no constant condition. Thus, he who can modify his tactics according to the enemy's situations shall be victorious and may be called the Divine Commander.

The Japanese have long ago discovered Sun Tzu's *Art of War* – Musashi Miyamoto's *Go Rin No Sho* or *Book of Five Rings* written some 370 years ago, is very much influenced by Sun Tzu's works. It is thus not surprising that some 40 years back, Japanese automakers had already initiated the production of cars with left-hand drive or right-hand drive for overseas markets while their American counterparts were then still arguing their heads off on whether to do so. Thereafter, the Japanese went further into the minute details of adjusting and shifting whatever necessary gadgets to accommodate the different driving requirements of the markets that they were selling to.

No doubt Sun Tzu has said:

Skillful warriors of ancient times first sought for themselves an invincible position where they would await for the opportunity to strike at their enemy's vulnerability.

But this does not mean waiting forever. For those CEOs who reject complacency, such waiting is only temporal and is stimulated by a planned course of aggression. In entering the Japanese market, Coca-Cola suffered a full decade of red ink but today it has a 60 per cent share of the soft-drink market in Japan. Many other American firms had discovered that it is not that impossible to do business with Japanese firms if one has a lot of patience and persistence. It may take some years of regular visitation before one can land a few small orders. But once confidence is gained, the trickle of orders could become an avalanche. This is certainly not a job for the complacent executive.

When our casualties increase, withdraw. If our force is so much weaker than the enemy's, we should totally avoid him for if a small army is stubborn, it will only end up being captured by the larger enemy force.

少則能逃之
不若則能避之
故小敵之堅
大敵之擒也

4
A Stubborn CEO Risks Becoming A Donkey

LET US FACE it – each one of us can be quite stubborn at times. Depending on the mood that seizes us, we can become most obstinate and thus behave in an irrational manner. It is no wonder then that at such times, we usually end up making donkeys of ourselves. And when the stubborn one happens to be the CEO, then the situation becomes even worse.

This is what Sun Tzu has to say about stubbornness:

> *When our casualties increase, withdraw. If our force is so much weaker than the enemy's, we should totally avoid him for if a small army is stubborn, it will only end up being captured by the larger enemy force.*

From this saying, you can gather that I am hitting out at the negative aspect of stubbornness and not its more positive version, i.e. doggedness, as exemplified by Sony's CEO Akio Morita who stubbornly stuck on to his decision to go ahead with the manufacture of a miniaturized, portable, personal hi-fi against objections from everyone else. He was proven right later when the Walkman raked in huge profits. However, in this case, Akio Morita knew what he was doing and it has nothing to do with his ego. Besides, far from being complacent, his very action was driven by his ceaseless pursuit for his organization's growth.

The Terrible Trio

We have already seen how arrogance, ignorance and complacency can lead a CEO astray. The terrible trio further appears to be behind that stubborn streak in a CEO. As Sun Tzu has warned:

> *There are five dangerous faults which a general should not have in his character. Recklessness leads to destruction; cowardice ends in capture; quick temper enables you to make him look foolish; delicate in honor causes sensitivity to shame; overly compassionate for his men exposes him to worry and harassment. These five faults in a general can seriously ruin military operations.*

I learnt very early about the danger of stubbornness when in 1972, as a secondary-school student (like most other teenagers, in the process of acquiring knowledge, are 'half-baked' and yet thinking oneself to be a 'know-all'), I was hospitalized at the University Hospital in Kuala Lumpur for an eye surgery.

A fellow patient, an undergraduate at the nearby University of Malaya, invited me to play a game of chess with him. I obliged and soon we had a good game going. Then, when I used my bishop to check his exposed king, thinking there is no way he could escape, he switched the positions of his king and castle by moving the former three spaces to the right and the latter two spaces to the left. I exploded: "Hey, what are you trying to do?" He looked at me calmly, and said: "This is a move called 'castling'". In my ignorance and to some extent, arrogance (after all, don't forget, I was then at the age where I just can't be wrong), I told him angrily: "You're fooling me. I've played chess all these years and never have I heard of such a move". He looked at me for a while, and again very calmly, he put the chess pieces back to their original positions and said: "Okay, you win this round. Shall we continue with another game?" We did but somehow the earlier happy mood was lost.

The years went by and something nagged at my sub-conscious mind until one day when I was back in Kuala Lumpur working as a journalist, I went to the office library and pulled out a book on chess to read. I then realized what an ass I had made of myself to my fellow patient that day at the University Hospital. Even till today, how I wish I could have the opportunity to meet up with him again so that I could tell him: "I owe you an apology. There is indeed such a move called 'castling' in chess but I have been an extremely ignorant and stubborn ass that day".

The Stubborn CEO

But how many people out there, especially CEOs who, in their stubbornness, have not yet learned to apologize even after finding out that they have erred in one way or other? Or worse, they may even conveniently shift the blame to others, especially those in subordinate positions.

When the CEO of a chain of supermarkets was invited to head a productivity drive in his country, he wanted to prove he could lead by example through launching an immediate courtesy campaign in his own outlets. One of his senior managers advised against such a hasty and unplanned launch, saying: "We're not ready as yet. Let us first provide some training for the staff and only then could we launch the courtesy campaign". He even went to the extent of quoting the following Sun Tzu's saying for the benefit of his CEO:

> *More planning shall give greater possibility of victory while less planning, lesser possibility of victory. So how about without planning?*

But the CEO stubbornly refused on the ground that they did not have the luxury of time. At the CEO's insistence, large, beautiful posters were printed and put up in every corner of the chain's stores, announcing the courtesy campaign. Although the posters succeeded in gaining the attention of shoppers, the campaign subsequently failed because the then expectant customers who were usually quite tolerant of the chain's normal poor service, became even more agitated when the staff failed to live up to such promises of courtesy. And of course, the senior manager got the blame!

Stubbornness can Slow One's Action

And in the business arena, many more CEOs have been known to cling stubbornly to decisions which may be proven wrong by subsequent events. For example, there is always some inertia effect from previous strategies which means prior strategies tend to influence current strategic choice and thus may result in certain alternatives not being explored even when the situation demands so.

Take the case of Ever Ready Limited. After establishing itself in the 1970s as the market leader in the zinc carbon batteries, it was unperturbed when Duracell which has been developing the alkaline-manganese batteries, began supplying the UK market from its Belgian plant in 1979. As Ever Ready stubbornly decided against developing its own alkaline-manganese batteries, an unopposed Duracell rapidly gained market shares. Finally, in 1983, only after falling profitability grew to crisis proportion that Ever Ready decided to bring out its own alkaline-manganese batteries. They could have learned from Sun Tzu who says:

Speed is the essence of war.

Over in the continent, the Centre Electronique Horloger in Neuchatel, Switzerland, discovered the quartz movement in 1967. The Swiss watchmakers were thus well placed to exploit and dominate the electronics technology but in their cling to the traditional mechanical movements in which so many decades and so much fixed investment had been sunk, they allowed the Japanese onslaught to cause nearly half of Switzerland's watch-making firms to disappear in the 1970s. It was fortunate for them that they had a leader like Ernst Thomke to rally them in a counter-attack through a watch with electronic accuracy but with the appeal of Swiss traditional dial and hands, and the kind of price which consumers had come to expect from the Japanese.

Be Ready to Listen

How then to avoid making donkeys of ourselves through being stubborn? Let us turn to Sun Tzu who says:

Know your enemy, know yourself and your victory will be undoubted. Know earth, know heaven and your victory will be complete.

The answer is knowledge – of those persons you are in contact with (employees, clients, competitors, suppliers, etc.), your own self, the market, the environment as represented by politics, economics, society and technology. And as I have advised in the last chapter, knowledge can only come if you are prepared to be like a sponge – ever ready to ask questions, listen, absorb and thereafter act fast on the information.

And when it comes to listening, pay heed to the observation of Stephen Covey, who writes in his book, *The Seven Habits of Highly Effective People*, that good listening comes about only when we are prepared to "listen with the intent of understanding as against listen with the intent of replying. Most times, we are either speaking or preparing to speak".

Through listening with the intent to understand, you may even pick up more businesses along the way. This is what Joseph Ranieri, the managing director of Universal Instruments Corporation (Singapore) Pte Ltd has to offer: "Start by opening up your mind. Accept that you could not be right all the time. Always be willing to listen to what the other person has to say. By being open-minded and willing to listen to my clients rather than stereotyping them, I have over the years, been able to understand their needs and found opportunities to satisfy those needs profitably".

Networking

And it is thus appropriate that here, we shall turn to the following of Sun Tzu's sayings:

> *A general is like the spoke of a wheel. If the connection is tight and complete, the wheel will be strong and so*

will be the State; if the connection is defective, then the State will be weak.

This is just a reminder to all CEOs on the importance of net-working, i.e. to be 'connected' to others. To listen, you will need sources who are ready to share their knowledge, experience or views, and networking could be one effective yet inexpensive way of gathering the necessary information.

Conformation to the terrain is the soldiers' best ally in battle.

夫地形者

兵之助也

5
Inflexibility is When the Donkey Also Wears Blinkers

IN THE LAST chapter, we saw how a stubborn CEO could behave like a donkey. And like the donkey who knows no other direction but straight ahead, especially when made to wear blinkers, the CEO who is inflexible, also could see no other option except that which he sets out to see.

Here, you can see that while being stubborn is an occasional lapse subject to our many moods, inflexibility tends to reflect a more inherent trait in our character. Thus, while a stubborn person can yet be flexible on other issues at other times, an inflexible person will tackle all issues with the same rigidity even though they may all be irrelevant to one another.

Throughout his book, Sun Tzu writes incessantly on the need to be flexible and his words could be applied to the following manifestations of inflexibility in a CEO.

On Competing Abroad

We hear a lot about globalization these days. But it is pathetic the way some of the CEOs go about their business. To them, globalizing seems to be nothing more than planting their national flags in the foreign host countries and then doing things the way they are being done back home, thus missing out on what Sun Tzu advocates:

> *Conformation to the terrain is the soldiers' best ally in battle.*

And to conform, one must be flexible, or be like "water" as Sun Tzu advised:

> *Military tactics are similar to water... As water shapes its flow according to the ground, an army wins by relating to the enemy it faces. And just as water retains no constant shape, in war there will be no constant condition. Thus, he who can modify his tactics according to the enemy's situation shall be victorious and may be called the Divine Commander.*

As Sun Tzu's works were introduced to Japan as early as 700 AD, the Japanese who are known to be very detailed and thorough in their planning, are not surprisingly, also very flexible when it comes to executing the plans. For example, unlike American products sold in overseas markets which are often priced in line with the home prices, the Japanese sold their television sets at very low prices when entering the US for the first time. They only raised the prices closer to the American models only after the Japan-made products had gained the consumers' acceptance.

But for the majority of American firms which are not so adept at being flexible when operating across geographic or cultural boundaries, there are yet companies like 3M subscribing to a slogan that permeates all their foreign subsidiaries: "Think global, act local". As a result, their executives are capable of acting locally in terms of marketing and selling which require flushing out the distinctive needs of each market they operate in, without losing global focus in manufacturing, distribution, and customer service so as to achieve the required levels of critical mass for costs and value.

On Fast Response to Changes

Sun Tzu says:

> *Speed is the essence of war. Take advantage of the enemy's lack of preparation; move by using unexpected routes and attack where he has made no defence.*

To do any or all of these, again, one must be very flexible so as to be able to speedily change one's ways of doing things.

When flushed with its initial success of gaining 37% market share against Honda's 38%, Yamaha's CEO Koike jubilantly announced in 1981, the opening of a new factory that would within a year make Yamaha the leader in the domestic market and number one in the world by the second year. Honda, in concentrating on its car sales, had most of its best people already working on the four-wheelers. But after learning of Yamaha's threat, Honda's CEO Kawashima counter-attacked by getting his people to work on and introduce 81 new models within a span of 18 months. Yamaha could only produce 34 and the Japanese motorbike wars thus ended with Koike admitting he had underestimated the enemy and thereafter leaving the company.

Any CEO who has a tendency to be indiscreet like Koike, should learn from Sun Tzu who says:

The supreme skill in commanding troops is in the shapeless command. Then, the prying of the subtlest spies cannot penetrate for the laying of plans against you.

As for Honda, the company was able to counter-attack effectively because it is renowned for its highly flexible production system with its shop floor being organized in a flexible manner so as to capitalize on changes in product designs and its workers trained to perform more than one function.

On Committees and Hierarchy

And when the decision-making authority comes in the form of one or more committees or levels of hierarchy, the inevitable inflexibility can be disastrous. Hence, despite launching its sporty two-seater Pontiac Fiero, General Motors could still not realize its dream of beating its Japanese. The car had design defects such as an engine which was underpowered for a genuine sports car. Even then, sales were initially promising as the model found appeal with young women who asked for power steering. Suffice to say, GM's hierarchy would not permit the necessary investment. Besides, there were far too many committees to reckon with. The result: the Fiero was a failure.

On Hiring of Capable People

As a fellow Sun Tzu's disciple, Quek Swee Lip has written in his book, *Business Warfare*, the aim of recruitment is to add strength to the organization and not to introduce cancers.

But from my personal observation as a 'headhunter', I find many CEOs are rather inflexible in their hiring decisions for their organizations. Even if the hiring is decided at lower levels, the CEO would have spread his cancer since the executives concerned would most times merely be engaging in the game we know so well – 'follow-the-leader'.

What I am hitting out at, are the two inflexible mindsets of these CEOs which could lead to cancers like losing the opportunity to get a real good guy for an organization or creating an artificial staff shortage. The first is what I have called, the mind in the 'functional' box which means a total refusal to consider anyone if they have not worked in a similar function. For example, not hiring a person for a job in the H.R. Department just because he has all along been working as a sales person. The second is the mind in the 'industry' box, where the reasoning goes like this: "If all these years, this guy has been working in the banking industry, what makes him think he could do well in our hotel industry? No, let's reject him".

Such thinking runs contrary to Sun Tzu who says:

> *A skilled commander selects his men according to their talents and uses them to exploit the situation.*

One such commander was my former boss, Michael Gian, at Kentucky Fried Chicken Management Pte Ltd. In late 1991, he dared to appoint me as his Director of Operations despite my not having any experience then in fast food operations. As Michael told me later: "I want someone who is objective and comes in with fresh ideas. Had I hired someone from, say McDonald's, he would end up 'McDonaldizing' our operations". During my tenure, we saw a marked improvement in our customer service as evidenced in the Survey Research Singapore's findings from our 9th position (1991) to 3rd (1992) to 2nd (1993) among all the fast-food chains in Singapore. On top of this, we enjoyed annual sales growth of 15 per cent and in the last year of my service, we achieved a net operating profit before tax of 25 per cent.

Indeed, people can be very versatile. We could learn from John Sculley who spent the first 16 years of his working life with PepsiCo before moving on to make a name for himself at Apple Computers. Or how about advertising executive Mitchell Fromstein who became CEO of Manpower, the world's largest temporary services concern? Much closer to home, we have Cheah Kim Teck, former general manager of McDonald's Restaurants Pte Ltd in Singapore, who is now general manager (Sales & Marketing) for Cycle & Carriage Industries Pte Ltd – certainly a change from selling hamburgers to luxury cars but it is not impossible.

But the CEO who has truly proven his acute insight into the fact that people can be very versatile is none other than Jimmy Lai, the Hong Kong-based founder of the Giordano casual wear group. About a year ago when he launched the Chinese-language newspaper, *Apple Daily*, he hired more than 10 pizza delivery boys to be reporters, saying: "We feel that now with the worsening traffic jams, pizza delivery boys know how to arrive at the spot the fastest...The details can be chased by other reporters". This is one man who sure knows his priority and I was told the *Apple Daily* is today's the most popular Chinese-language newspaper in Hong Kong.

On Utilizing Personnel

Although hiring people should be done without the inflexibility described earlier, their subsequent utilization must be more proper and prudent because of the three ways of bringing misfortune to an army, Sun Tzu identifies one of them as:

> *By using the army officers without discretion, when ignorant of the military principle of being flexible with the circumstances. This causes doubts in the minds of the officers.*

Take myself for example. After Michael Gian had hired me as director of operations, while he could and should at times involve me in discussions of marketing or financial issues so as to tap my input and also keep me in the picture, he must never allow me to handle or worse, interfere in marketing or financial decisions. Even though I had experience in marketing and hold a qualification in accounting and finance, I am not hired for those portfolios. He already has a director of marketing and a director of finance handling those jobs and if I were allowed to run loose in their areas of responsibilities (as some CEOs are known to permit or even encourage such indiscretion), the organization would very likely be reduced into a free-for-all internal battlefield in no time.

*It is the business of a general
to be calm and mysterious;
fair and composed.*

將軍之事

靜以幽

正以治

6
Could He Really Be The CEO?

AFTER YEARS OF climbing up the corporate ladder, when an executive suddenly finds himself in the exalted role as CEO in his organization, there is the danger that he may yet forget himself. As scores of new CEOs discover each year, becoming a CEO entails much more than a change of jobs, or assuming new responsibilities, or even joining a better country club. It requires a total change in the new CEO's lifestyle and even dictates the way he behaves.

To quote Sun Tzu:

> *It is the business of a general to be calm and mysterious; fair and composed. He must be capable of mystifying his officers and men so that they are ignorant of his true intentions.*

A New Set of Rules

Being mysterious and to mystify one's staff often require some degrees of deception, which as Sun Tzu observed:

> *All warfare is based on deception. Therefore, when capable, pretend to be incapable; when active, inactive; when near, make the enemy believe that you are far away; when far away, that you are near.*

Deception here is not meant to be devious but simply means you just cannot be your true self anymore – saying whatever that comes to mind or behaving the way you usually do.

This was what my former boss, Dato' Lim Chee Wah, the senior general manager of Malayan Sugar Manufacturing Company Berhad told me so many years ago: "It's like you have become two persons and the real you is kept hidden from public eyes. You just cannot afford to be your old self and let your hair down in public. Instead you play by a completely new set of rules".

The new set of rules means watching and controlling virtually every aspect of his public behavior which explains why he always sits upright, walks straight and speaks only after due thought and in a calm and steady manner.

Watch What you Say

The new CEO will learn to put his personal interests aside for the corporate good and one of the first rules is watching what he says. After all, as the new CEO, you represent not just yourself but the corporation as well. When people discusses you, they are discussing you in the same breath as the corporation you represent. And if you are not too careful in what you say, everyone lower down will simply seize onto every word you utter. It is thus worthwhile to pay heed to the following advice which Sun Tzu offers:

Subtle and secretive, the skilled general learns to be invisible and silent to control the enemy's fate.

Wise words indeed. Had the commander of the US forces in the Pacific, Admiral Richard Macke not uttered aloud his opinion (especially to the Press) that the three US servicemen who allegedly raped a 12-year-old Japanese girl in Okinawa should have instead hired a prostitute, he would not have to suffer his forced retirement in November 1995. As a high-ranking officer, his words carried much weight and would be seen as the policy of the entire US military command which explains why the other top brass chose to distance themselves from him.

Watch What you Do

Most CEOs will also learn that they cannot afford any controversy. As a CEO's personal interests are too easily confused with his corporation's, he needs to watch his actions. For example, you may not want to be seen or even photographed raising a mug of beer lest such a sight alienates employees or shareholders or community members who frown on alcohol. This disciplined honing down of sharp edges – at least in public – could be what Sun Tzu had in mind when he writes:

The good commander seeks virtues and goes about disciplining himself according to the laws so as to effect control over his success.

In this area, most CEOs should put a renewed premium on emotional control since losing one's temper or even cursing aloud is frowned upon as quite unbecoming of a leader. This again brings to mind Sun Tzu's warning that:

> *No ruler should put troops into the field just because he is angry; no general should fight because he is resentful. Move only when there is benefit to be gained, quit when there is no more advantage. For an angry man can later become happy, a resentful man become pleased, but a kingdom once destroyed can never be restored nor the dead be brought back to life.*

Hence, although like any other person, you can be personally angry, nonetheless do refrain from angry outburst against your employees or even business competitors in public. Lord King of British Airways was angered over Virgin's access to Heathrow and in his petulance, he reportedly referred to Richard Branson, the chairman of Virgin Atlantic Airways, as a 'pirate.' Not only was Branson motivated thereafter in his crusade to unseat British Airways as the 'world's favorite airline', but Lord King's outburst also gave the former much public sympathy and free advertising to the detriment of the latter (and British Airways) in terms of credibility.

Watch Who you Fraternize With

As the act of keeping a discreet distance from one's subordinates has become an inevitable ritual among new managers, CEOs are even more vulnerable. True, the great strategist advocated forming alliances but he further warned:

> *If we cannot fathom the designs of our neighboring States, we cannot enter into alliances in advance.*

As a seasoned CEO confided to me: "From the moment I became the top man, colleagues and others began flocking to me like moths to a flame. People that I never even knew or had met only briefly in past years and who would perhaps have a hard time figuring out who I was from meeting to meeting, suddenly remember who I am. Surrounded by favor seekers and sycophants, I soon learned to question the motives of all those I come into contact with. And when my first crisis at the helm came, I realized it's helluva lonely up there".

Sometimes, the need to keep reasonable distances from subordinates arises because you do not want to give people the wrong message.

Shortly after a business development manager joined my company, she succeeded in talking one of her former colleagues to join her team. I soon noticed the two of them often went out for lunch together and I advised her that by socializing with one subordinate and not another, she risked sending wrong messages to the ones she does not see. They may feel she does not like them or will not promote them, etc. She thought I was being petty until one day when she froze all leave applications due to exigencies of business and got some funny stares from her staff that she suddenly realized her friend had several weeks prior to the emergency, already applied for and gotten her approval to go on leave that very day.

This has been covered by Sun Tzu when he writes:

> ... if a general is too indulgent; if he loves his soldiers too much to enforce his commands; and cannot assert control when his troops are in disorder, then the soldiers are similar to spoilt children and shall become useless.

While this saying reflects Sun Tzu's warning about the practice of favoritism, it further reinforces the fact that a CEO who can keep a discreet distance from his subordinates, will ensure everyone could see him as a fair and unbiased leader. The desirable end result is that while you should be as informal and open as possible in the office, do not promote social relationships outside the office, especially with the opposite sex.

Watch How you Dress

Upon switching from being an advertising executive to taking over the reins at Manpower in the mid-1970s, one of the things Mitchell Fromstein did was to throw out the flashy clothing of the advertising world. He realized that what looks good inside the advertising industry would be too frivolous for the big, worldwide temporary-services concern.

Likewise, as my wife told me back in 1989 when I became general manager of Metroplex Holdings Sdn Bhd managing The Mall shopping complex in Kuala Lumpur: "You must stop dressing sloppily lest you run into somebody and you can't afford to let them think you're a slob". She did not add but we both knew her next unspoken sentence: "Or that The Mall is sloppily run".

Then again, in 1993, while I was at the Times Bookshop at Marina Square shopping mall in Singapore, my wife excitedly nudged me: "See, that man has just picked up your book". I retorted that he could be just browsing and would not necessarily buy. Nonetheless, we trailed that man throughout his stay at the store and when he finally paid for the book at the counter, I was so moved (it was the first time I actually saw someone buying my book) that I wanted to go up to him, announce myself and offer to autograph the book for him. But my wife stopped me short: "Take a good look at yourself first". I was in my weekend garb – shorts, T-shirt, rubber slippers and a head of unkempt hair. This could probably happen had I done what I proposed to do – the guy would very likely gawk: "You, the author. Good grief, excuse me, Miss, I would like a refund, if you don't mind".

So this is how a general ought to be – calm and mysterious; fair and composed. Do you still begrudge the high pay and perks your CEO is enjoying?

A general is like the spoke of a wheel. If the connection is tight and complete, the wheel will be strong and so will be the State; if the connection is defective, then the State will be weak.

夫將者，國之輔也。輔周則國必強，輔隙則國必弱。

7
Breathing Down Subordinates' Necks

SUN TZU DESCRIBES three ways whereby a ruler can bring misfortune upon his army:

> *By commanding an army to advance or retreat, when ignorant on whether to advance or retreat... By trying to administer an army the same way he administers a kingdom, when ignorant of military affairs... By using the army officers without discretion, when ignorant of the military principle of being flexible with the circumstances.*

All three instances smirk of an interfering CEO who has nothing better to do than to breathe down his subordinates' necks by turn. Let us look at each of these situations.

Knows Not, Interferes Got

As Sun Tzu said:

> *By commanding an army to advance or retreat, when ignorant on whether to advance or retreat.*

In the same way, this was how an executive contemptuously described his boss to me: "knows not, interferes got", meaning a CEO who, despite his gross ignorance, is yet most eager in wanting a say in everything that his subordinates are doing. From what I was told, nothing in the company where the executive was working in could get done without the said CEO's personal approval. From placing an advertisement in the classified section of the local newspaper to the confirmation of an employee about to complete his probation, all must have the CEO's endorsement. There are indeed many such CEOs out there.

It's Quite Simple... Everything's Done this Way

Let us refer to Sun Tzu's words again:

> *By trying to administer an army the same way he administers a kingdom, when ignorant of military affairs.*

Many modern-day management gurus have emphasized the need for a CEO to be capable of taking the 'helicopter' view. Thus, it is sad to find that there are yet CEOs out there who would insist on taking a narrow view. Very often, such CEOs are specialists in their own respective field, e.g. finance or marketing, etc., before moving up to their exalted position as the CEO. This is why I used the word 'sad' to describe the situation: these CEOs could be first-rate in their own narrow functional area but they have never matured into the wider responsibilities of managing the total business as expected of them at the CEO level.

A good example is the financial controller who finds himself elevated into the CEO's office. He would start his reign by telling everyone to cut costs and in pushing all other issues aside, would personally take the lead by scrutinizing the figures himself and calling on each person to explain or justify any item which he could not figure out. Or how about the marketing manager who, upon becoming CEO, could see nothing more important than the four Ps – product, price, place and promotion? These CEOs simply cannot bring themselves to let go. Either their professional craft-pride blinds them to the real faults in the organization or in clinging to their 'safe' area of specialization, they just refuse to see that their craft is but just a part of the whole problem.

A Free-For-All Situation

This is what Sun Tzu warned:

> *By using the army officers without discretion, when ignorant of the military principle of being flexible with the circumstances.*

In one large retail chain, the CEO has a tendency to get his executives to perform jobs which are not within their direct scope of responsibility. For example, although he has a general manager (with several years of retail experience) in charge of retail operations, he would nonetheless direct all the monthly reports from the various store managers (who reports directly to the general manager of retail) be channeled to another general manager who has responsibility for planning. And when the said general manager for planning was later directed to take charge of a turnaround exercise for the company-owned restaurants, to his surprise, he found a committee headed by the human resource manager, in existence, to question any of his initiatives. In the said organization, everyone seems to be doing the other person's job.

This tactic should not be confused with Sun Tzu's teaching but is really the more ruthless 'divide-and-rule' tactic taken right out of another book, *The Prince* by Niccolo Machiavelli (1469-1527) whose famous treatise on statecraft was regarded as downright wicked that at one time the author was identified with Satan himself. Despite its title, Sun Tzu's *Art of War* actually takes a more positive approach as we shall see.

Need for Empowerment

Although in recent years, we have been hearing a lot about 'empowerment', it is interesting to note that some 2,500 years ago, Sun Tzu has already made this call:

> *Put your men in positions where there is no escape and even when facing death, they will not run. In preparing for death, what is there that cannot be achieved? Both officers and men will do their best. In a desperate situation, they lose their sense of fear; without a way out, they shall stand firm. When they are deep within the enemy's territory, they are bound together and without an alternative, they will fight hard. Thus, without the need of supervision, they will be alert, and without being asked, they will support their general; without being ordered, they will trust him.*

I believe this could be Sun Tzu's way of describing empower-ment because I interpret his words to mean we should refrain from coddling our subordinates through taking over all their work problems. Instead, we should trust their capability to take responsibility in fending for themselves and thus, encourage them to sort out their problems themselves. But as Gan Thian Leong, the CEO of the Brunsfield Group in Malaysia told me: "Such refrain from interfering with how our subordinates per-form their work does not mean being ignorant of what is going on or totally without providing some guidance to them when needed". True, for as I have quoted Sun Tzu previously:

A general is like the spoke of a wheel. If the connection is tight and complete, the wheel will be strong and so will be the State; if the connection is defective, then the State will be weak.

Do not interfere but remain in touch. Hence, should any of my managers come to me with their work problems, instead of taking over by telling the manager what to do, I would rather hear him out, prompt him with pertinent questions which are meant to make him see the situation more clearly, and then, let him decide on what course of action to adopt. Of course, if I have any doubt over his proposed action, I would have already talked it over with him in the first instance during our dialogue session.

Empowerment – A Very Abused Concept

Empowerment is certainly the key. But really, empowerment is a very abused concept.

It was in 1957 that Douglas McGregor first espoused Theory X – the assumption that people are generally indolent, not ambitious and thus, dislike responsibility, resulting in bosses adopting a 'let's-tell-them-what-to-do-and-then-watch-them-like-a-hawk' attitude towards employees and thereby resorting to punitive measures to get productivity from them. McGregor is obviously rooting for Theory Y – that is, people being capable of self-direction and self-control, could therefore be more motivated through being entrusted with responsibility – the very essence of empowerment.

But today, despite a span of four decades, many bosses are still on the Theory X track although professing to be Theory Y managers. While one may sometimes still get some productivity from the Theory X approach, I cannot help asking whether a Theory Y approach may not have reaped even better results. After all, the great strategist has this to comment on the use of punitive measures:

> *Too frequent punishments show the general to be in dire distress as nothing else can keep the soldiers in check. If the officers at first treat their men harshly and later fear them, then the limit of indiscipline is reached.*

Hence, we find many CEOs today are merely paying lip-service to empowerment. Since many management gurus have been talking about it, and the word has quite a sophisticated ring to it, naturally it has become hip and fashionable to include this word as part of one's daily vocabulary. Besides, it also enhances one's image as a progressive, modern boss. But really, only a small fraction of today's CEOs have truly recognized the potential power in empowering their employees. One such CEO is Stan Shih of the ACER Group where employees are accorded due respect as shareholders and thus regarded as bosses. This surely beats the practice of many American companies where empowerment may just equate to subordinates being allowed to call their bosses by first name but when it comes to getting things done, it's "no go without my saying so!"

Then, there are yet those CEOs who see empowerment as delegating away complete authority to their subordinates who are thereafter expected to take over the worries, sweat and tears as well. However, the catch is that these CEOs still regard their status as their God-given right and therefore, are entitled to keep any of the glory and the honor earned in 'bloody battles' by their subordinates. It is no wonder that executive turnover in organizations with such CEOs tend to be high as the common complaint is: "I just can't stand a boss who would stoop so low as to steal credit for my ideas or my effort".

By moral law, I mean that which causes the people to be in total accord with their ruler so that they will follow him in life and unto death without fear for their lives and undaunted by any peril.

道者
令民与上同意
故也可与之死
可以与之生
而不畏危

8
Even Afraid of One's Own Shadow

THE FEARFUL ORGANIZATION could never be a dynamic one. Much of the dynamism would be lost when everyone (from the office cleaner right up to the CEO himself) starts to fear a tiny failure, impending retrenchment or whatever the kinks may be.

Such an organization would be lacking the 'moral law' which Sun Tzu has described as:

> *By moral law, I mean that which causes the people to be in total accord with their ruler so that they will follow him in life and unto death without fear for their lives and undaunted by any peril.*

And in cautioning against the five 'dangerous faults,' cowardice is one of them:

> *There are five dangerous faults which a general should not have in his character... cowardice, which ends in*

capture... These five faults can seriously ruin military operations.

In contemporary times, management guru Tom Peters has this to say about 'fear' in his book, *Thriving on Chaos*: "Until fear is erased or minimized, hustle – urgent testing of the untried – will not become common. Information hoarding rather than sharing (information is power, after all) and action-delaying tactics (not to act is not to risk failure) become the norm in fearful organizations. Political maneuvering (in an effort to make oneself apparently valuable to someone who looks like a survivor) goes up too".

So Who is to Blame?

Sun Tzu clearly blames the general because in his book, he writes:

> *When troops are inclined to flee, insubordinate against commands, distressed, disorganized or defeated, it is the fault of the general as none of these calamities arises from natural causes.*

In the same manner, we can also blame the CEO for the fear in his organization. The probability of his being scared, even of his own shadow, is very high.

The Fearful CEO

When a CEO became overly cautious in taking a decision, his behavior is quite similar to what I have come to observe as the average investors' behavior when the 'bear' makes its retreat in the stock market. As the index starts plunging and prices fall, making it a good time to pick up stocks, the average investor would simply stay clear for fear of even grosser disaster. The average CEO is really no different – he fears taking a decision that runs contrary to the general view because he fears that others may know more than he does. And since everyone is so adept in the 'follow-the-leader' game, it is no wonder that fear becomes the norm once a CEO behaves that way. In such organizations, it is common to hear: "I'm afraid it won't work..." or "I don't think the top man will approve..." or how about, "as it has never been done this way before, so I don't think I should..."

Doing the Unexpected

Instead of following the crowd (more people need not necessarily be right), there are times when it pays to be different by doing the unexpected. As Sun Tzu has wrote time and again:

> *Attack where the enemy is unprepared; appear where you are least expected...*

and,

> *...Appear at those places that he must hasten to defend; move swiftly to those where you are not expected...*

and again,

> *...When I wish to avoid a fight, I can prevent an engagement even though the battlelines had been drawn by diverting my enemy with something odd and unexpected thrown in his way.*

To illustrate this strategy of doing the unexpected, let me share this ancient Chinese story with you: During the Three Kingdoms Period (220AD to 280AD), a phased withdrawal of the

Shu's army left premier and commander-in-chief Zhuge Liang with only a fraction of his troops. It was then that scouts reported the coming of a large troop of enemy soldiers under Wei's commander-in-chief Sima Yi. Instead of preparing to defend, Zhuge Liang ordered all the four gates of the city opened wide, the soldiers changed into civilian clothes and sent to sweep the streets while he personally went up to the main tower to play his lute. Sima Yi could hardly believe his eyes, and fearing an ambush, hastily beat a retreat which enabled Zhuge Liang to escape.

Not Afraid of Making Mistakes

Sun Tzu has shown he values courage in a general for he has identified this trait as one of the five virtues which a general must cultivate:

> *By command, I mean the general's stand for the virtues of wisdom, sincerity, benevolence, courage and strictness.*

In 1953 when James Burke first started with Johnson & Johnson, he was by far too imaginative. Feeling the company was too centralized, stifling and lacking a new-product department, he left after a year. Three weeks later, he was asked back to head the very department he had proposed. One of his first stabs at innovation was a children's chest rub which failed dismally and he was summoned to the presence of General Robert Wood Johnson, the company's awesome chairman who asked: "Are you the one who cost us all that money?" Fearing the ax, Burke nonetheless admitted, only to be told: "Well, I just want to congratulate you. If you are making mistakes, that means you are making decisions and taking risks. And we won't grow unless you take risks". Burke went on to become CEO of Johnson & Johnson.

When someone who knew the general well heard this story, he commented that if Burke had made another blunder after the first, his second stay at Johnson & Johnson would sure as hell have been shorter than his first. This principle would be very much in line with Sun Tzu's call:

> *The skillful general neither requires a second levy of conscripts nor more than one provisioning...*

and,

> *He [a skillful fighter] wins by making no mistake. Making no mistake means already having established the certainty of victory; conquering an enemy who is already defeated.*

In June 1995, in an interview, the *Straits Times* quoted Y.Y. Wong, the founder and chairman of Singapore's WyWy Group, as saying: "I tell my guys, you are allowed to fail, failure is the licence to try. If necessity is the mother of all creation, then I think failure is the step-mother of all new inventions". It is no wonder then that his business machine distributorship has pushed deeper into the regional markets and ventured into new high-growth sectors such as lifestyle.

Not Afraid to Take a Stand

In 1957, when Sony created the first pocket transistor radio, the firm's co-founder, Akio Morita took the new wonder to the USA where it attracted the interest of Bulova, the then great watch company. Bulova ordered 100,000 pieces (staggering to the then infant Sony) on the condition that the radios carry Bulova's name. As Morita refused, the Bulova man went on to insist: "Our company is a famous brand which took over 50 years to establish while nobody has ever heard of your brand. Why not take advantage of ours?" Morita replied: "Fifty-years ago, your brand must have been just as unknown as our name is today. I am here with a new product, and I am now taking the first step for the next 50 years of my company. Fifty years from now I promise you that our name will be just as famous as your company name is today".

It took Sony only 30 years to become one of the premier multinational companies with a brand name that, attached to any electronics product, is enough to command a premium price. If Morita had been a fearful negotiator, Sony would merely remain a 'sonny' today instead of the 'Sony' we know.

Not Afraid to be Unpopular

The following warning is found in Sun Tzu's book:

> *If a general is too indulgent; if he loves his soldiers too much to enforce his commands, and cannot assert control when the troops are in disorder, then the soldiers are similar to spoilt children and shall become useless.*

There are CEOs who prefer popularity to effectiveness. Such CEOs fear to hurt their employees' feelings. In this way, you can say they carry the concept of being nice to the extreme simply because they want to feel loved by their staff. It is thus not surprising that such companies often tend to be ineffective since they carry more 'passengers' than 'sailors'. These are the 'country club managers' – those with low concern for productivity but high concern for people – identified by Robert Blake and Jane Moulton in their famous concept, the Managerial Grid.

Try this extreme case for example: in one American firm where I was once interviewed for a general manager's position, the expatriate CEO told me that he found me "larger than life" and my dynamism could cause some discomfort to the other team members (who happened to be a few junior staff already hired). He suggested that I should meet up with them to enable them to feel (and thereafter provide feedback to him) whether they would be comfortable with me. Always game for experiences, I agreed and after suffering a postponement by the busy business development executive who was assigned to 'interview' me, I finally met the team comprising the latter and his two subordinates. In the midst of the interview, he disappeared for some 30 minutes to return an "urgent" pager call, leaving me to his subordinates. I suppose they (the business development executive in particular) must have found me too overwhelming to be their boss for I did not hear from the CEO thereafter. But on reflection, I was grateful for the experience because had I joined this organization, I could see there could be no end of troubles since the CEO seems to worry more for the team's happiness than the corporate effectiveness which the general manager is hired to accomplish.

So, if ever you feel fear gripping you, remember what former US president John Kennedy once said: "Our fears must never hold us back from pursuing our hopes".

More planning shall give greater possibility of victory while less planning, lesser possibility of victory. So how about those without planning? By this measure, I can clearly foresee victory or defeat.

多算勝
少算不勝
而況無算乎

9
Happy Are Those Who Dream Dreams

TWENTY-TWO YEARS AGO, I left Penang to study in Singapore. When I first stepped into my hostel room, I saw a poster whose words have greatly influenced my life ever since: "Happy are those who dream dreams and are willing to pay the price to make their dreams come true". Indeed, every dream carries a price. And if you are unwilling to pay that price, you are just a mere dreamer ... maybe, even a frustrated one at that.

Great CEOs are those who would dream great dreams and then proceed to pay the price to make their dreams come true. They are the visionaries who would spare no effort to see to the realization of their visions. The average ones may dream but either could not manage well enough or simply lack the determination to see their dreams bear fruit. Then there are yet those who would merely dream but beyond that, nothing more would take place.

The Strategic Implications

For dreams to come true, planning is just one of the price tags to consider. Sun Tzu realized this when he first wrote the following words in his book, *Art of War*, some 2,500 years ago:

> *More planning shall give greater possibility of victory while less planning, lesser possibility of victory. So how about those without planning? By this measure, I can clearly foresee victory or defeat.*

But there are certain pitfalls facing CEOs when it comes to planning as we shall see.

Recklessness

Unlike the fearful CEO, who, in applying the brakes on his organization's dynamism, can prevent its progress and growth, a reckless CEO bent on throwing caution to the wind can do even greater harm. Such CEOs either fail to plan at all or they would just rush recklessly into a venture, armed only with a 'half-baked' plan.

Recklessness is one of the five dangerous faults which a general should not have in his character as Sun Tzu warned:

> *...Recklessness leads to destruction...*

and he gives the following advice:

> *...Always observe and assess the situation before making your move...*

and

...Hence, the enlightened ruler is prudent and the good general should not be hasty. Thus, a country is safe and the army preserved.

In 1990, Kentucky Fried Chicken launched its US-driven Colonel's Country Breakfast project in Singapore. Its massive advertising campaign succeeded in bringing in eager customers to try out the breakfast products but poor operational delivery as evidenced in cold, salty, or over-fried food, out-of products' situation, and slow service provided by the stressed-out serving crew later resulted in many customers swearing off their patronage. The breakfast program was eventually withdrawn in 1993. It was a lesson that functions like operations and marketing must never hastily go each other's way but ought to be coordinated for effective delivery. Moreover, an appreciation of the differences among people and cultures is essential.

Slowness

On the other hand, we could find the other extreme – slowness. Here, the typical CEO seems to believe he has all the time in the world. Such CEOs would be well-advised to read the following of Sun Tzu's words:

Victory is the main object in war. If this is long delayed, weapons will become blunt and the ardor of the soldiers will be dampened...Thus, while we have heard of stupid haste in war, we have not yet seen a clever operation that was prolonged. History has shown that there has never been a country benefiting from prolonged warfare.

His advice? Just this simple and straight-to-the-point observation:

Speed is the essence of war.

But unfortunately, there are yet many who would ignore this advice. One such case was the four-year delay in the decision of Ever Ready Limited to develop the alkaline-manganese batteries despite having been alerted to Duracell's move in 1979. It was only in 1983, after falling profitability grew to crisis proportion due to an unopposed Duracell which had rapidly gained market share, that it decided to bring out its own alkaline-manganese batteries.

Indecisiveness

Planning is futile if in the end plans are never executed due to the indecision of the planner or planners. This must be why Sun Tzu pointed out that:

The enlightened ruler plans well ahead, and good generals serve to execute the plans.

Once, I experienced my shortest ever career as a general manager. For some five-and-a-half months, I was enthusiastically drawing up plans for my boss but due to his vacillation, most of the plans merely gathered dust on his table. Despite my constant reminders, he just could not decide. And worse, given his untrusting nature, he would not allow anyone else to do anything without his personal approval. In my frustration, I quoted an ancient proverb to him: "If you suspect a man, don't employ him. But after you have employed him, don't suspect him". Thereafter, I handed him my resignation letter and moved on to better pastures and greater challenges.

Of course, most indecisive CEOs are often quick to say (as did my boss) that they are merely trying to ensure everything is exactly right before taking any action. If you still remember my last discourse on the fearful CEOs, then you will recognize this to be just an excuse. As a result of such lame excuses, many large, institutionally-run companies have allowed opportunities to pass them by. It is thus heartening that there have been exemplary CEOs like Konosuke Matsushita and Soichiro Honda who were known for their decisiveness in executing their chosen plans regardless of any minor shift in circumstances.

Long-term vs Short-term Planning

In April 1996, Singapore's banker Wee Cho Yaw was reported in the *Straits Times* as saying that there is a tendency of today's business strategies to emphasize the short-term than the long. The chairman and CEO of the United Overseas Bank Group said he once asked the general manager of a foreign bank why he was so generous with his loan terms in Singapore. The latter said he wanted to build up a big portfolio during his term so as to show his head office that he was generating profit. From this answer, Wee believed that the quality of the loans was of secondary importance to the general manager since bad loans normally take time to surface, by which time he would have finished his term, leaving the bad loans to the luckless successor to handle.

I certainly agree with this observation as I have personally seen managers who, in dedicating themselves to laying the foundation for the future, were subsequently passed over for promotion because their bosses were more enamored with those who could show more immediate results albeit short-term ones.

To quote Sun Tzu who also emphasizes the need for long-term planning, he makes the following recollection from ancient Chinese history:

> *In ancient times, when Yin succeeded Hsia in power, it was due to I-Chih who as the chief minister of Hsia was responsible for the State's affairs; then when Chou succeeded Yin, it was Lu Ya the former Minister of Yin, who helped Chou to construct the solid foundation for a glorious dynasty of twenty-nine generations.*

In ancient times, rulers who plan ahead for a long-lasting rule, takes the people's interest into consideration, i.e. if we still recall Sun Tzu's moral law. Today, people would mainly comprise employees and customers. As Philip Kotler of Kellogg School of Business at Northwestern University noted in his book, *Marketing Management*: "...too many US corporate leaders focused their attention on the stock market and not enough on the real market... they pursued profits first and customer satisfaction second".

Seek Originality

Visionary CEOs tend to be original in their approach. Somehow, I find this tendency to be in line with what Sun Tzu advocated:

> *To foresee a victory that others can also foresee is no great feat. There is no greatness in winning battles and being proclaimed universally as an expert, for to lift a rabbit's hair requires no great strength; to see the sun and the moon is not a sign of sharp sight; to hear the thunderclap is not a sign of sharp hearing.*

Originality need not be something totally new. It is just being able to see from another angle and do something differently. For example, while flying military missions in Vietnam, Fred Smith was already thinking how he could take over the postman's job once he hit civvy street. With his famous 'hub-and-spoke' concept in mind, he went on to build Federal Express into the world's largest air freight company which today dominates the overnight delivery business with a market share in excess of 50 percent. Part of the price he paid must have been those sleepless nights when the company initially soaked up US$80 million in outside money (excluding several million of his own) before it started to make a profit.

Be in Control of your Dreams

Finally, be in control of your dreams. As Sun Tzu said:

> *Skillful warriors of ancient times first sought for themselves an invincible position where they would await the opportunity to strike at their enemy's vulnerability.*

Again, I have found this to be true of the truly successful CEOs today. They are not contented to wait for things to happen. Instead, they are always aiming for positions from which they could dictate the moves – based upon their own will and not in response to the moves as dictated by others. Take Singapore's Senior Minister Lee Kuan Yew for example. He told 250 journalists and diplomats at a dinner talk in June 1996 that his generation had built Singapore by pursuing their ideals based on "a democratic society, keen and vibrant, a united people, who, regardless of their race, language and religion, and based on justice and equality, achieve happiness, prosperity and progress for the nation". In his words: "We did not focus our minds on our navels or we would have missed the rainbow in the sky. We pursued that rainbow and that was how, together, we built today's Singapore". He was referring to his then generation's fight for independence from colonial rule and subsequent breakaway from Malaysia.

Over the causeway, in Malaysia, Prime Minister Dato Seri Dr Mahathir Mohamed is another example of visionary leadership. Instead of allowing Malaysia to slide into being a Third World nation and waiting meekly for the West to offer 'handouts', he led the country to its heights with his visions of a national car, double-digit economic growth and Vision 2020. Perhaps, this could be what Sun Tzu was trying to tell us when he first wrote:

...the skillful commander imposes his will on the enemy by making the enemy come to him instead of being brought to the enemy.

The average and mediocre CEOs (and sadly enough, there are plenty of them around) would rather wait and see what their rival is doing and then counter or emulate it. Hence, we find many firms whose policy has been to see what their competitors do and then copy whatever is being done. Sounds familiar? If so, then it is high time that you review your approach.

Without harmony in the State, no military expedition can be made; without harmony in the army, no battle formation can be directed.

含英咀華

立和而寀

10
How Reliable Are Your Trusted 'Courtiers'?

A LONG TIME ago, when I was still in primary school, I saw a Teochew stage opera where a general was maligned by an emperor's favorite eunuch. Despite the protests of the Prime Minister, the Emperor subsequently ordered the general's execution. I was perplexed then – was not the Prime Minister higher ranked and therefore more powerful than the lowly eunuch? I was given an answer which left me even more confused – yes, the Prime Minister held a higher rank but the eunuch was more influential and thus more powerful.

Today, after having worked in the corporate world for more than 16 years, I understand the concept very well. As I have written in my book, *Applying Sun Tzu's Art of War in Corporate Politics*, like ancient times when court intrigues could destroy a general's career regardless of his valor or strategic brilliance on the battlefields, today's managers may yet find their careers plagued by negative corporate politics.

Generals vs Courtiers

Call it 'line and staff' if you wish but I prefer to view it from the Teochew opera perspective of 'generals and courtiers'. There appears to be a running battle in most corporations between these two sets of key players. As a management consultant, I have often heard frustrated sales managers, short of salesmen and caught in an intensely competitive situation, bemoaning: "As if I haven't got enough to worry about... yesterday, I got a memo from head office demanding twelve pages of statistical returns, and now came this other memo telling me to cut down the expense claims of my salesmen and do a head-count". In such situations, it is inevitable that generals would view courtiers as impractical 'smart alecs' who need to serve time at the 'battlefields' to find out for themselves what 'getting bloodied' is really like, while courtiers on the other side, tend to regard generals as an irresponsible, indisciplined and perhaps, dim-witted lot.

The Role of the Ruler or CEO

The link between the two warring factions would be the ruler or what we now have come to know as the CEO. His is a balancing act and it pays for him to remember the following saying of Sun Tzu:

> *Without harmony in the State, no military expedition can be made; without harmony in the army, no battle formation can be directed.*

Harmony is the key but sad to say, not many CEOs can balance well. All too often, he tends to veer towards valuing the courtiers more than the generals. After all, courtiers are closer on hand while generals are more often out and away at the 'battlefronts'. Courtiers may also become indispensable to the CEO since their existence often serve to supplement some of the CEO's deficiencies, e.g. administration or information technology which requires the courtier to follow through and implement some sort of system based on what the CEO's wants, employee or public relations where another courtier may be more adept in handling people tactfully and saying the right things to the Press, etc.

An Internal Value System

Any disharmony between the 'generals' and 'courtiers' would be bad for Sun Tzu warned:

> *Those skillful commanders of old knew how to split the enemy's unity between the front and rear troops; to prevent cooperation between the main force and the reinforcement; to hinder the stronger troops from rescuing the weaker ones, and subordinates from supporting their superiors.*

And disharmony shall certainly be the result when a CEO cannot balance well by listening to only one or a few executives and ignoring the rest. This is Sun Tzu's caution against favoritism:

> *If he is too indulgent; if he loves his men too much to enforce his commands; and cannot assert control when the troops are in disorder, then the soldiers are similar to spoilt children and cannot be used.*

One way to effect this balancing act is to impose an internal value system which prioritizes the importance of generals whose efforts (or lack of it) on the 'battlefronts' will determine whether the organization will be safe from or vulnerable to the enemy's attack. This does not mean courtiers are less important but on the contrary, such a system will prove their importance only if they contribute towards the success of the generals. In other words, CEOs should view courtiers as providers of service to the internal customers, i.e. the generals, and accordingly strive to get this message across. Only then can the CEO be impartial and thus bring harmony to his team.

Hands-on Management

Another way to effect the balancing act is to get courtiers to spend a short time in the 'battlefields' just to experience what it is truly like. We have already heard so much about job rotation in Japanese organizations which provide opportunities to their employees to learn about relationships among different jobs, thus fostering understanding and goodwill. As the Japanese way may be too time-consuming, a short-cut approach is to incorporate the experience into the induction training. For example, during my time with Kentucky Fried Chicken in Singapore, all employees, as part of the induction training, were required to spend time serving in restaurants, learning how to fry chicken, prepare coleslaw and of course, mop the toilets. Even at my level as operations director, I was not spared. Thus, I was delighted indeed to read in the *Straits Times* in early 1995 that the management staff of the Royal Sporting House led by its CEO, V.K. Gomber, were sent to do front-end selling. The same report also told of the financial controller having to sweep the shop floor. This is good practice so long as one is careful not to over-do it.

Check out the Facts Yourself

No CEO should attempt to do everything himself but ought to delegate effectively through empowering his managers. This is certainly in keeping with the following Sun Tzu's observation:

Those who do not use local guides cannot benefit from the advantages of the ground.

Here, I shall take local guides to mean those department heads who should be experts in their respective functions and capable of exercising their judgment. But, as and when possible, a CEO should still be astute enough as to check out certain facts for himself especially if the feedback tends to be negative. As Sun Tzu has said:

Only the one who is wise and sagely, benevolent and just, can use secret agents. Only he who is sensitive and subtle can get the truth out of their reports.

One scarce resource in today's corporate world would be good managers. But sometimes the fault lies with the CEO who after hearing of some talented persons, would delegate to his HR manager (or any other executive) to conduct the initial interview. While there is nothing wrong in such delegation (since the CEO may not have the time), it is quite unfortunate that many CEOs would simply accept the reports (especially the negative ones) from their managers as final. Good reputation does not come easy and it is my belief that the more negative the report is about someone who is reputed as talented, the greater the need that it ought to be checked out by the CEO himself. It may turn out that the manager concerned is biased, or has not bothered to look beyond the surface, or simply is afraid of the more talented newcomers subsequently edging him out of his boss's favor. Given the common complaint of a shortage of talent, I think such CEOs deserve it if they, in over-relying on the judgment of their favorite courtiers, eventually lose the services of capable people.

When the Boys from Regional Office Come A-Visiting

Those who are working for the local office of a worldwide multinational would inevitably experience the 'once-a-while' visit from a courtier of the regional office. If you are a CEO of a regional office, then it is very important that you take the following saying of Sun Tzu to heart if you do not wish to lose good people in the offices covered in your region:

> *A general is like the spoke of a wheel. If the connection is tight and complete, the wheel will be strong and so will be the State; if the connection is defective, then the State will be weak.*

Be directly connected to some of the executives in those offices so that should you hear any negative report from your managers making the rounds in the region, you could check out the facts yourself. I have personally suffered because of a regional manager who, whenever he visited Singapore, would come to office just in time for lunch, then go through the motion of conducting a meeting for a couple of hours (during which time he would yawn very often) and by 5 p.m. sharp, would make a beeline for his hotel, after extracting a promise from some of the local managers to entertain him to dinner and make the rounds at the night spots. As I was stupid enough in not entertaining him, he maligned me to his boss, the regional CEO. The result: despite two years of excellent ratings in my annual performance appraisal by my immediate boss, the regional CEO (who could

112

not be bothered to check the facts) threw so many spanners in my direction that eventually I left the organization.

As you can see, I certainly found out the hard way, after all these years, why the Prime Minister in the Teochew stage opera, was less influential and powerful than the eunuch despite holding a higher rank than the eunuch. And, the poor general, of course, ended up dead. But the story, to my ultimate delight, has a perfect ending: when left without good generals and an impotent Prime Minister, the factuous Emperor perished in his burning palace during an invasion by hostile barbarians. Take care that you do not end up like this Emperor.

When positioning an army to observe the enemy, cross over the mountains and stay close to the valleys. Position yourself on high ground with a wide view.

吧雲軍相敵

絕山依谷

視坐變高

11
Miss the Forest for A Tree

WITH HARDLY A doubt, a CEO should spend more of his time thinking about the big issues and long-term changes which will either bring growth or ferment decay to various parts of his organization. And he should do this by taking the 'helicopter view' which some modern-day management gurus have called, or 'mountain view' as Sun Tzu would be wont to call it. At least on two occasions, he writes in the *Art of War*:

> *When positioning an army to observe the enemy, cross over the mountains and stay close to the valleys. Position yourself on high ground with a wide view.*

And later in the book, he repeats:

> *Choose a high position with a wide view.*

This emphasis on the wide view is to enable a CEO to grasp the situation thoroughly so that he could avail himself to more strategic options. After all, as Sun Tzu has observed:

One who does not thoroughly understand the calamity of war shall be unable to thoroughly comprehend the advantage of war.

As such, the principle still stands whether in 500BC or in the 21st Century – at the CEO's level, he should be more concerned with strategic issues and thus it is not for him to fuss over the day-to-day problems.

When Top Managers are into Petty Issues

But the strange thing is: while nine out of ten persons can tell you this fact, yet how often we still hear of boards of directors spending hours discussing insignificant issues like priorities for the allocation of car-park lots when they move into the new building, or some other equally petty issues? Okay, fair enough, we can take the words of Robert Waterman Jr that the board functions really as a club and a paid one at that. But then how about those supposedly no-nonsense managers who would often deliberately hold a meeting down to trivial issues because that is all they can cope with? In either case, I am very sure that Sun Tzu would point accusingly at the CEO because he already advised:

When one sets in motion an entire army to chase an advantage, the chances are that he will not attain it.

So, as a CEO, let your managers cope with the waves but keep your watch on the tide instead.

When Small could be Big

Yet, even if he is not blinded by the small issues, a CEO must still watch against being blind to the small details. Thus, in his grander quest for those great schemes, he must still ensure that no issue (no matter how tiny) escapes his notice. This is because a small thing may yet carry greater implication. As Sun Tzu has warned:

> In battle, having more soldiers will not necessarily secure victory. Never advance by relying blindly on the strength of military power alone... But anyone who lacks consideration and treats the enemy with contempt and disdain will only end up being captured himself.

For example, whenever the festive season is just around the corner, and it is time to send Christmas and New Year cards to those people we know, this common mistake will happen: I have personally noticed that many CEOs are fond of sending out greeting cards without personally signing them. Do you think your name embossed in gold or an imprinted rubber-stamped signature is good enough? You are only fooling yourself because such an insignificant act clearly reflects a larger (and lasting) impression: your lack of consideration, and perhaps a touch of arrogance. And when I pointed out this folly to those CEOs I know, interestingly, they were often unaware that they have done such a thing. This is what I mean by not paying attention to the small issues.

But this one surely beats the lot. In 1992, I received a rubber-stamped Christmas card from the general manager of a town and country club. I scribbled a short message on the card to point out that it is better to send a signed card than a rubber-stamped one, and returned it to him. A week later, he replied, offering the excuse of "too many cards to send" but nonetheless, promising to review his approach. Gratified, I sent him an autographed copy of one of my books as a personal gift. When I failed to hear from him after a month, I telephoned to ask if he had received the book. He acknowledged having received the book and apologized for not replying as he was very busy. A week later, I got a "thank you" card, signed on his behalf by his secretary!!! This must be one very overworked town and country club's general manager. I hope he is compensated well for being so overworked.

Negative and Positive Consequences

Just to rub home my point on how small issues could lead to bigger consequences, let me share the following stories with you:

When a local firm invited the sales manager of a luxury car company to make a sales presentation, upon visiting the firm, he was brought to the general manager's office. Although there was a young lady sitting in the room, the general manager did not make any formal introduction (informality is often the practice of some Asian family-run companies) and the sales manager proceeded to exchange business cards with the general manager. He did not offer his card to the young lady who, later he found out, was the daughter of the firm's owner. As the firm's executive director, she was also the immediate boss of the general manager who was negotiating for a car for her use. The snub (as she perceived it even though the sales manager swore it to be an oversight) led her to subsequently decide on a car from a rival sales manager who showed her more consideration and courtesy of acknowledging her presence with a card.

While this story only resulted in the loss of a deal, how about this other one which resulted in the loss of a life? In May 1996, the supreme commander of the US Navy, Admiral Jeremy Boorda committed suicide hours after he learned that *Newsweek* magazine was investigating why he was wearing two Vietnam War combat decorations with a "V" insignia (signifying valor for combat) when he was only awarded the ones without the insignia. In his suicide note, he described his action as "an honest mistake". Mistake it may be, but tragically, it ended his life.

In another incident, a senior manager observed some workers in his factory gathering amongst themselves and talking in low tones. Whenever any supervisor went near, they would disperse but later would regroup and continue their whispering. As a student of Sun Tzu's war principles, he recalled the great strategist's words:

When troops are seen whispering amongst themselves in small groups, the general has lost the confidence of his men.

The manager investigated and found out that the supervisor of this group of workers had initiated several policies of his own which not only contradicted the company's but were extremely harsh on his staff. As they perceived the supervisor to be management, they regarded the policies to come from management and thus developed a general resentment towards the management. An eye for details and quick action thus saved the company from a potential strike which could have developed if the group had been influential enough to gain the sympathy of other groups.

Then, there was this revelation by Singapore's Senior Minister Lee Kuan Yew: in his early years of nation-building, the small island-republic was able to woo foreign investors because of its well-kept trees and gardens. To quote some of his words, "These were CEOs... so when they drove along Orchard Road and turned into the Istana, without a word being spoken, they knew that this place works. The grass has got to be mown every other day, the greens have to be cut daily, the trees have to be tended, the flowers in the gardens have to be looked after... so they know this place gave attention to detail".

Beware of What is Obvious

When one is capable of taking in a wide view and still be aware of the tiny details, he should be more secure against being deceived by what is obvious. The following is a famous advice given by Sun Tzu:

All warfare is based on deception. Therefore, when capable, pretend to be incapable; when active, inactive; when near, make the enemy believe that you are far away; when far away, that you are near. Hold out baits to lure the enemy; feign disorder and strike him.

Therefore, anyone can just hop on and play this 'deception' game. It therefore pays to be wary. The great strategist has this additional piece of advice to offer:

Do not pursue an enemy who pretends to flee.

And be wary of "Excellence"

Much has been written about excellence ever since Tom Peters and Robert Waterman, Jr first wrote *In Search of Excellence*. But long before them, in fact too long even to be remembered, the Chinese already has this saying about excellence: "If excellence can be attained, then it is probably not worth having". Why is this so? For an ancient answer, I must again, repeat the following of Sun Tzu words:

In battle, having more soldiers will not necessarily secure victory. Never advance by relying blindly on the strength of military power alone.

This is certainly a warning against complacency which is the inevitable consequence whenever one thinks one has achieved excellence. Here, let us reflect on a modern answer as found in the Singer Sewing Machine Corporation which, after decades of prosperity and success and international fame, started to slide into a terrible decline in the 1950s. Donald Kircher who then came in as president to lift the company out of its mess, said: "Its very success led to the assumption that all the answers were found, and that all one had to do was do what one's predecessors had done before. Everything became ingrained. There were no outside influences acting on the Company. It became withdrawn into itself".

The remedy? At the risk of repeating myself, Sun Tzu has this to offer:

The good commander seeks virtues and goes about disciplining himself according to the laws so as to effect control over his success.

Have enough self-discipline to scrutinize yourself (and your actions) with a critical eye. At your level as a CEO, while you must not be blinded by the petty issues and refrain from interfering unnecessarily with your subordinates' work, you must yet watch against being blind to the small details.

*By command, I mean the
general's stand for the virtues
of wisdom, sincerity,
benevolence, courage and
strictness.*

將者

智信仁勇嚴也

12
Morality Or The Lack Of It

IF YOU HAVE been faithfully following me so far, you should realize by now that Sun Tzu's *Art of War* is more than a book about formulating military strategies, leading and motivating troops to win wars or in contemporary times, managing one's business successfully. The book carries heavy undertones which are mostly about how to live one's life virtuously, i.e. the act of being moral.

The *Webster's Dictionary* defines moral as that:

1. pertaining to the principles of right and wrong; and
2. in accordance with standards of right conduct, i.e. being virtuous.

Sun Tzu has indeed cautioned generals against immorality:

When the general is morally weak and lacks authority; when his instructions are not clear; when there are no consistent rules to guide both officers and men, and the ranks are slovenly formed, the result is disorganization.

This clearly explains an earlier observation in the *Art of War*:

When troops are inclined to flee, insubordinate against commands, distressed, disorganized or defeated, it is the fault of the general as none of these calamities arises from natural causes.

Thus, being a general so long ago or being a CEO today certainly carries heavy responsibility. And to live virtuously, Sun Tzu offers the following advice:

The good commander seeks virtues and goes about disciplining himself according to the laws so as to effect control over his success.

Let us first look at some of the negative scenarios.

When the General is Morally Weak and Lacks Authority

In December 1995, the *New York Times* reported the conclusion of a navy inquiry whereby the deputy commander of NATO forces in Spain and Portugal, Rear-Admiral Ralph Tindal, was involved in an inappropriate year-long affair with an aide. After the 55-year-old Naval Academy graduate and 35-year veteran was found guilty of adultery, fraternization, conduct unbecoming of an officer and sexual harassment, he was given a punitive reprimand, fined a month's pay of about US$7,700 and placed under house arrest for 30 days. Instead, he requested for early retirement and was subsequently demoted one rank to one-star admiral and left the navy in early 1996.

When Instructions are not Clear or Lack of Consistent Rules

An expatriate regional CEO told his newly-hired local manager of the Singapore office: "As I trust all my employees absolutely, of course, I trust you since you're looking after this country for me". But when the latter bought some computer softwares to replace the illegal ones in the office, the CEO was most displeased and insisted that the expenditure must get his personal approval otherwise "don't buy". And when the year's financial performance subsequently showed a marked improvement over the prior year's, the manager's request for a mere 5 per cent annual increment for his staff, was rejected. In ordering further downsizing, the CEO explained: "We're still in the red and therefore, we should refrain from spending unnecessarily". Two months later, when the manager resigned, the CEO felt it necessary to transfer over another expatriate manager and thus incur the spending of a hefty sum on housing and car, etc., just to maintain him.

When Ranks are Slovenly Formed

In defining his fifth fundamental factor of "doctrine", Sun Tzu says:

> *By doctrine, I mean the way an army is organized in its proper subdivisions, the gradations of ranks among the officers ...*

Written some 2,500 years ago, but today, even though supported by a contemporary Henri Fayol's classical hierarchy with one man at the top, with three or five below him, and each in turn, has another three or five below, etc., we still find organizational structures which are inappropriate for the strategic direction or tasks which need to be performed. Without clear lines of direction, sloth appears to be the order (or disorder) of the day.

The Five Virtues of a General

Sun Tzu has a very simple advice to offer and by now, you should be most familiar with the following of his words:

> *By command, I mean the general's stand for the virtues of wisdom, sincerity, benevolence, courage and strictness.*

In this final round-up, let us reflect on each of these virtues.

Wisdom

A wise CEO is always open to new ideas even if such ideas were to come from the lowliest of his employees. In his wisdom, he learns to shun arrogance (e.g. believing himself to be a 'know-all') and he realizes there is a vast potential of learning from others with the result that he listens and he learns. It is just as Sun Tzu said:

> *Be subtle, be subtle, and you can use espionage anywhere.*

The key word is anywhere, which also means anyone. Far too many managers have made the mistake of taking the following stand: "Why should I take your advice? If you are so clever, how come it's me and not you who sits on my chair?" The end-result: in their arrogance, they never consider seriously what their subordinates tell them and so they learn nothing at all.

Sincerity

In May 1996, both Reuter and AFP reported the resignation of Datuk Salleh Said Keruak as the chief minister of Sabah, a resource-rich Malaysian state in line with a promise made during the 1994 state election to share the post with the state's three main ethnic groups. In his words: "I have been consistently saying I will go when the time comes. I don't want allegations that when you have become comfortable in the job, you want to cling on to it". Interestingly, this was carried out despite opposition from some members of his party, Sabah UMNO (United Malay National Organization), who fear the appointment of a non-Malay to the post may jeopardize Malay interest in the state. Datuk Salleh is indeed 'the precious jewel of the State' which Sun Tzu has extolled:

> *Thus, the general who advances without coveting fame and withdraws without fearing disgrace but whose sole intention is to protect the people and serve his ruler, is the precious jewel of the State.*

This is one way to express sincerity: keeping your word. I wish more CEOs in the corporate world would emulate Datuk Salleh's example because sadly enough, there are many lofty mission statements and pledges of quality floating about but without actual delivery of their promises.

Sincerity is also about being truly concerned towards others and being responsible for them, especially those who are in your charge. Take the case of another Asian politician who, despite being publicised widely for her self-righteousness, could yet hardly hold a candle to Datuk Salleh. I usually tend to admire the courage of opposition politicians who are usually "underdogs" when standing up against established governments. But when I read of this particular politician making appeals to foreign governments to impose economic sanctions against her own country and urging foreign businessmen to cease investing in her country, I cease regarding her as 'the precious jewel of the State'. If true, such actions would only hurt her countrymen more. In the corporate world, the actions of this politician would be no different from those of an executive who, being unsuccessful in his bid for power, would thereafter ask customers not to buy from his company or tell competitors to take away his company's market share. Such a person would hardly have any thought about how his actions could hurt his fellow employees.

Benevolence

It was the benevolent nature of CEOs like Dave Packard and Bill Hewlett (e.g. their inherent dislike of time clocks to keep employees' time) that laid the lasting foundation for Hewlett-Packard. In Singapore, for example, out of 62 employees who first started out with HP in 1970, 48 still remain today. Its newly appointed managing director in Singapore, Cheah Kean Huat told the *Straits Times* in May 1996: "The secret of our success is still people. If you get that right, everything else follows". This is very much in keeping with Sun Tzu's observation:

Such a general who protects his soldiers like infants will have them following him into the deepest valleys. A general who treats his soldiers like his own beloved sons will have their willingness to die for him.

This is indeed the essence of benevolence but of course, in today's context, we will not want our men to die for us. As C.T. Chua, the vice-president of SCI Manufacturing in Singapore told me: "Just go that extra mile will do". And as he leads by example in going round the plant and visiting his people at work, it

132

is no wonder that his managers do the same. The same can be said of Philip Ng, the Managing Director of Far East Organization who would board a company's bus every Saturday morning with his executives to go round and see his organization's many construction projects. This way, he not only shows his interest in his people at work but also reflects his personal determination to deliver quality homes to his customers.

Courage

Still remember my earlier discourse on the fearful CEO? Then, you could see why a CEO who lacks courage will not make effective decision. Even if he could eventually come to a decision, it would be too late. After all, Sun Tzu has this to say about timing:

> *Whenever the enemy presents an opportunity, take it quickly.*

But opportunity waits for no man and once the opportune time has passed by, there goes the opportunity. Apart from the courage to decide, a CEO must not be afraid to take on opposition. This means no 'yes-man' culture. This is in line with the following Sun Tzu's advice:

> *If the situation offers victory but the ruler forbids fighting, the general may still fight. If the situation is such that he cannot win, then the general must not fight even if the ruler orders him to do so.*

As the few potential leaders in any community usually tend to make uncomfortable and at times, disagreeable subordinates to their bosses, they may thus end up being described as "too individualistic", "argumentative", or even "egocentric". As they are not likely to be obedient, at least not all the time, and may go their own way in getting things done as they feel reasonable (which is unreasonable in their bosses' perception), it is sad that when it comes to promotion, they are often passed over. As a result, many organizations have lost great people. And the stage for future decay is set since more docile, obedient and easy-to-handle subordinates are promoted instead.

Strictness (or Discipline)

It is pointless to enforce discipline on others when you cannot toe the line yourself. Hence, instead of running amuck in enforcing his new-found power over others the moment one becomes CEO, look to lead by example instead. I know one CEO who would often take his executives to task over their expense account but when it comes to entertaining himself or even his personal friends and relatives, there is absolutely no limit. And having installed CCTVs all over the workplace and getting security guards to monitor the movement of the employees (even general managers are not spared), he would also question his executives on their time-keeping or going out of the office. But he comes to office around 10.30 a.m. and would often disappear even for weeks to attend to his personal matters. And unknown to him, he is really the laughing stock of the company as his staff would joke endlessly about him. Or how about those other CEOs who would abuse their positions of authority by insisting on their, usually female employees, to work late and then, by the way, have dinner with them. This is a subtle form of sexual harrassment.

Admittedly, all of us are not born perfect. But having been blessed to reach such a high station in life as a CEO, we must strive all the more to lead an exemplary life. As Malaysian Deputy Prime Minister Datuk Seri Anwar Ibrahim rightfully urged in September 1996, corporate leaders must help to draw up a code of ethics to make them socially responsible. According to him, a corporation has no soul to be summoned before God and has no body to be flogged. Hence he warned: "Unless corporations are prepared to assume greater responsibility in protecting the environment, improving public health and morality, promoting equity and social justice, their future will be at stake".

It certainly takes lots of self-discipline to live up to Sun Tzu's principles which is why I have said the *Art of War* is more than military strategies, winning wars or managing business successfully... it is really about how to live one's life virtuously. In today's competitive 'battlefields' shaped by accelerating change, while we may still reign supreme in our own mini-kingdoms as CEOs where most or all of our subordinates may not feel up to telling us where we fail, it is worthwhile then to have Sun Tzu as the keeper of our conscience. The other alternative is, of course, to emulate those generals of the ancient State of Wu, who in discarding Sun Tzu's words of wisdom, caused the State to be exterminated in 473BC.

Index

Praises for the Author's Other Books

"...Khoo has managed to bring the whole subject to a most welcomed level of realism by injecting examples of actual management situations he has come across in his career... The most notable aspect of the book however is how Khoo has managed to translate what is a complicated treatise into a easily readable and, more importantly, understandable prose... All in all the book is certainly worth a read, especially for people in management."

Review of Sun Tzu & Management
by Gopal Sreenevasan
Malaysian Business (November 1992)

"The first in South-east Asia to link Sun Tzu's words to business in a 1989 book entitled War At Work, Penang-born Mr Khoo is known to take a more practical approach to Sun Tzu's principles, applying them to business with examples culled from his 15 years in management..."

Comments of Janet Ho
Straits Times (29/3/95)
after an interview with the author

"It is written in a breezy style and ought to appeal to those who find corporate politics mentally taxing."

Review of Applying Sun Tzu's
Art of War in Corporate Politics
The Sun (6/9/95)

"...he [Mr Khoo] does not advocate any underhanded or Machiavellian means. Instead, Mr Khoo shows how to apply Sun Tzu's 2,500-year-old strategies in a positive manner to improve working ties with colleagues."

Review of Applying Sun Tzu's
Art of War in Corporate Politics
by Chen Jingwen
The Straits Times (15/9/95)

"Peppered with real-life experiences, this book has succeeded in bringing hope to the reader... This is definitely a book you cannot afford to forgo."

Review of Applying Sun Tzu's
Art of War in Corporate Politics
by Kirsten Hughes
Certified Management Digest (February 1996)

Seminars

Many executives and organizations have attended the Author's seminars which range from a one-day or one-and-a-half-day *Management: The Sun Tzu Way* program to a two-day seminar cum workshop, or short three-hour to three-and-half-hour talks in various applications of Sun Tzu's *Art of War* to specific areas such as Management and Leadership, Marketing Strategies, Human Resource Management, Customer Service Management, Team-Building, etc.

WHAT THEY SAY:

"We have all been buffeted the last 30 to 40 years by ideas and concepts of management from the famous schools of business in England and the United States, and all of a sudden, we have in our own backyard, principles and management practices which are very similar."

K.B. Low
Managing Director
IBM, Singapore

"If a seminar is a form of drama, Mr Khoo had definitely displayed excellent showmanship."

The Management Development
Institute of Singapore

"After hearing Mr Khoo's talk, I decided that my executives must also hear him talk."

Gan Thian Leong
CEO
Brunsfield Group of Companies, Malaysia

"You brought to life the concept first written 2,500 years ago. Your real-life executive experiences are both vivid and current."

Paul Chan
Managing Director, Asia Pacific
Compaq Computer Asia Pte. Ltd.

"On behalf of the Polytechnic, I would like to thank you for your excellent presentation during last Saturday's seminar. It was well received, with many chief executive officers and senior executives finding the seminar interesting and enlightening. It was also an eye-opener for those who were hearing Sun Tzu's strategies and philosophies for the first time."

Bruce Poh
Director, International Development and Industry Services
Nanyang Polytechnic, Singapore

"We received very good feedback on the talk. Mr Khoo captivated the participants with his tongue-in-cheek style of delivery.

Singapore Institute of Insurance

If you are interested in engaging the Author to speak, please contact:

Stirling Training & Management Consultants Pte Ltd
128A Tanjong Pagar Road
Singapore 088535
Fax: (02) 2244933
E-mail: suntzu@pacific.net.sg